BIOGRAPHY OF

THE MAHARAJA

SRI RAM CHANDRA BHANJ DEO

Owing to the antiquity and rarity of this book, certain pages are regrettably absent, and readability is compromised due to the blurring of the original text. If you possess any insights regarding the availability of these missing sections, kindly inform us. Your assistance is crucial in ensuring the completion of this significant work for the benefit of future generations.

BIOGRAPHY OF
THE MAHARAJA
SRI RAM CHANDRA BHANJ DEO

SAILENDRA NATH SARKAR

Published by

FacsiMile Publisher
12 Pragati Market
Ashok Vihar, Ph-2
Delhi - 110052, India
Phone: 011-47034999
Email: www.facsimilepublishers.com
info@facsimilepublishers.com

Distribution Network
gyanbooks.com
India, USA, Canada, UK, Australia

ISBN: 978-93-6896-957-0 (PB)
First Published, 1918

2nd Impression 2025

Printed at: Gyan Press, Delhi.

BIOGRAPHY OF THE MAHARAJA SRI RAM CHANDRA BHANJ DEO
Author: SAILENDRA NATH SARKAR

BIOGRAPHY OF

THE

Maharaja Sri RAM CHANDRA BHANJ DEO

Feudatory Chief of Mayurbhanj

BY

SAILENDRA NATH SARKAR, M.A

Sir, Charles Elliot Gold Medalist

Head Master, Oriental Seminary, Calcutta

Calcutta

Published by The MAYURBHANJ STATE

1918

PREFACE

A FEW years of friendship quickly following on our first official relations and continued until his tragic and untimely end constitute my claim to preface the biography of Maharaja Sri Ram Chandra Bhanj Deo with a word of tribute to his clear and noble soul. In one sense it must have been an easy life to write for the character and the career were singularly free from complications. Born to be the head of a State, and, because he was very early left an orphan, destined to assume the duties of that position at the earliest possible moment, Sri Ram Chandra Bhanj Deo was trained for his future work by people with a high ideal of its demands; he accepted that ideal from the first and followed it to the end. No one similarly placed has ever been less distracted by conflicting standards of what is worth living for; least of all was he dazzled by the mere vanities and baubles offered so profusely and insistently to the wealthy and powerful. Many times in his life he must have had great difficulty in deciding the course he was to follow, but never any in taking duty as the touchstone to apply. The conception of a ruler as the first servant of his people is not new in India, nor is its practical application exceptional, though it is more general now than at some periods of the past; but certainly it has never had a more consistent exponent than the late Maharaja.

The mere material results of his all too brief rule give some measure of the industry and concentration which went to produce them. He was allowed only twenty years for his task. Certainly he had a fair start; when he took charge of his State it was already moving on the road by which he intended that it should travel. Other circumstances were favourable, he had perhaps to encounter less than usual of the opposition which all reformers must expect, for his people were loyal and docile, he had capable and faithful servants—that was all to his credit for they were mainly his own choice—

and sympathetic advisers in the successive political officers with whom he was in relations. His administrative career did not, of course, escape its share of the drawbacks incidental to all human enterprise. There were exceptions to the very general success of his undertakings. Some experiments failed, some things had to be begun over again, but the deductions due to these are trifling in comparison with the total sum. It may also be said that the Maharaja was less wedded to preconceived ideas and more ready to acknowledge error than the majority of those who are in a position to give practical effect to their own conceptions. When all favouring elements have been allowed for and all deductions made for cases of failure or incomplete success, the progress made in every direction in Mayurbhanj between 1892 and 1912 was beyond ordinary experience and such as could only have been attained by untiring industry and perfect singleness of purpose. His country grown from a rude jungle mahal to a prosperous and highly developed and equipped modern State, is Maharaja Sri Ram Chandra Bhanj Deo's monument, than which no man could desire one more splendid.

This appreciation of his public labours may have given an impression of extreme austerity and detachment from domestic interests. Nothing could be further from the fact. Sri Ram Chandra Bhanj Deo was deeply responsive to all the chords of human affection, and more than once had to suffer severely where he was most sensitive.

Babu Sailendra Nath Sarkar, who served him long and knew him well, has striven to give a faithful and sympathetic presentment of a fine character and has, I think, succeeded in producing one which will give pleasure to all who honour the pursuit of high ideals and will arouse the patriotic pride of Indians who have confidence in the will and capacity of their natural leaders to meet the demands of their high vocation.

F. W. DUKE.

AUTHOR'S PREFACE.

Sri Ram Chandra Bhanj Deo, the late Maharaja of Mayurbhanj, was a man whose private character and public life, whose amiable disposition, simple habits, charming and unassuming manners, profound scholarship, administrative ability, highmindedness and zeal for work, were such as to win the appreciation, regard and affection of all who knew him. In fact his character and career were such as to set a not unworthy example to others, whether of high or low estate, of a life well led and duty well done; and so with the object of making more widely known the facts of this life, and perhaps of inducing others to follow in his footsteps, Mr. B. Borroah, out of his admiration for and friendship with the late Maharaja, offered a handsome prize for the writing of his biography and undertook to defray all costs of its publication and translation from his own purse. Accordingly a Committee was appointed in the State to choose an author and approve of the book, and the Committee selected my humble self from among others, as I have some knowledge of the State, though it would have been better if a more competent man were entrusted with the task; for, I am afraid, that with my poor ability, I have not succeeded in doing full justice to the hero of the book. However, the book has been approved by the Committee, and is now published in the hope that it may meet with the appreciation of the public as an effort to do justice to and perpetuate the memory of a man whose ideals and achievements deserve to be widely known. I crave the indulgence of the public to overlook the faults and defects in style and idiom; for, after all, they should bear in mind that the book has been written by an Indian in a foreign tongue.

I cannot sufficiently express my heartfelt gratitude to Mr. C. L. Philip, M.A., I.C.S., the popular Superintendent of the Mayurbhanj State and President of the Maharaja Shri Ram Chandra Memorial Committee, for rendering me invaluable help, by kindly revising the book before publication, and lending me many official documents and records of the Mayurbhanj State from which to draw materials for the work.

I also beg to acknowledge my debt to Mr. L. E. B. Cobden Ramsay, I.C.S., C.I.E., for the help which I derived from his book entitled "Feudatory States of Orissa" ("Bengal Gazetteer," Vol. XXI). My best thanks are also due to Rautrai Sahib Sridam Chandra Bhanj Deo, brother of the late Maharaja, and to some officers of the State for supplying me with materials for the book.

S. N. SARKAR.

CONTENTS.

LIST OF ILLUSTRATIONS.

CHAPTER I.

A Brief Account of Mayurbhanj and Its People.

MAYURBHANJ, the Feudatory State in Orissa, of which the subject of this memoir, Maharaja Sri Ram Chandra Bhanj Deo, was Chief from 1882 till his premature death by accident in 1912, is a picturesque country. The hoary hills, mute witnesses of the mighty works of time, the lofty waterfalls and babbling brooks singing the song of eternity, the dark and deep sal forests sheltering all manner of wild animals, the cultivated valleys and plains, appeal alike to the artist and the man of action. The beautiful and interesting environment in which Sri Ram Chandra was born and lived, and the rich field for enterprise and development which his State afforded, contributed not a little to the growth of a character, the sympathy, conscientiousness, nobility and manliness of which earned the well-merited appreciation of all those with whom he came in contact. His interest ranged from the ancient history of the social and religious antiquities of the State to the most modern methods of its government and of the development of its resources. From the date of his accession almost till the hour of his death, his whole heart and soul were devoted to the improvement of his heritage and the amelioration and upraising of the condition of its people, and the success which he achieved was due in no small measure to his love for the country of his birth and his realization of the trust placed upon him.

The field of his endeavours was no small one and provided a variety of problems to engage his attention and absorb his energies. Mayurbhanj State is 4,243 square miles in area, and is the premier State in Orissa in every respect, in size, in population, and in income. It is bounded on the north by the Midnapur and Singhbhum districts, on the south by the district of Balasore and by the State of Nilgiri, on the east by Balasore and Midnapur, and on the west by Singbhum and Keonjhar State. It comprises within its boundaries every variety of soil and scenery. The vast tracts of jungles and the group of hills present a striking contrast to the smiling plains of Bengal, where every inch of ground yields some produce to the cultivator; but nature has compensated for this, not simply by lavishing her beauty but also by bestowing a portion of her mineral and forest wealth, the exploitation of which contributes considerably to the income of the State and to the support of its inhabitants, and will do so to a very much greater extent by careful management in the future.

The Simlipal group of hills, occupying an area of about 900 square miles in the centre of the State, has not yet been geologically surveyed, but is believed to be composed mainly of the oldest formation of crystalline and metamorphic rock. Portions of the rest of the State were geologically surveyed at the instance of the Maharaja and traces of useful and valuable minerals were discovered in various places. Of these the only one which has been commercially exploited on a large scale up to date is the iron ore which occurs in large masses of very good quality in the Bahmanghatti sub-division. The Tata Iron and Steel Company took a lease of the iron mines on the Gurumahisani Hill in 1911 and get from there the whole of their supply of iron ore.

Red and yellow ochres occur at places but so far have been used only by the local people. Mica is found in small quantities and of inferior size and quality. Further exploration is necessary to discover whether it exists in workable form and this was under the consideration of the Maharaja just before his death.

A yellow fossiliferous limestone occurs at Mahulia, two miles south of Baripada, but is not of commercial value, though of great interest to geologists. Pot stones and soap stones of good quality are found in various places and are manufactured into household utensils of different kinds and exported to Calcutta. Agate, flint, jasper, and other similar stones occur in the Bahmanghatti subdivision. The laterite, which covers large areas in the Sadar subdivision of the State, makes excellent building stone and the clay which underlies it is very suitable for some kinds of pottery.

Gold is washed in the Subarnarekha river on the border of Mayurbhanj, and in the Khadkai and Barhai rivers in the Bahmanghatti subdivision. There are alluvial deposits of gold at the head-waters of these rivers which provide a source of livelihood to a limited number of gold-washers of the State and neighbouring districts, but no native gold reefs have so far been discovered.

The forests of Mayurbhanj are valuable. Though large areas in the plains were ruthlessly destroyed in past generations, there are still considerable tracts of virgin and unspoilt forests in the Simlipal hills and other places. The policy of forest conservation initiated by the late Maharaja preserved these for systematic exploitation and ensured not only the preservation and continuance of the existing forests for commercial purposes and for meeting the household and agricultural needs of the people, but also contemplates the reafforestation of denuded tracts which are unsuitable for cultivation. Besides sal, which is the most prevalent, and commercially the most important tree, there are large areas of mixed forests containing such useful trees as Peasal

(Pterocarpus Marsupium) Sisu (Dalbergia Latifolia), Rohini (Soymida Febrifuga), Gamari (Gmelina Arboria), Karam (Adina Cordifolia), Assan (Terminalia Tomentosa), Champa (Michalia Champaka), and Kuchila (Strychnos Nux Vomica). Besides furnishing good timber, the forests provide large quantities of such miscellaneous products as myrabolams, nux vomica seed, kusum fruit, resin, charcoal, lac, tassar cocoons, simul cotton, tanning bark and medicinal roots and bark, the collection of and trade in which brings employment to large numbers of people and contributes considerably to the income of the State.

The State is well watered; the three main drainage areas being that of the Subarnarekha which touches the eastern boundary, that of the Baitarni which separates Mayurbhanj from Keonjhar on the west, and in the centre that of the Burabulang (great python), which has its source in the Simlipal hills and flows to the sea east of Balasore. The river system furnishes abundant facilities for irrigation of crops on a large scale, without which the continued fertility of the high lands cannot be assured. This fact was well appreciated by the Maharaja, who planned and carried out two large irrigation schemes and contemplated others of much greater magnitude. These will be described in more detail later. With the exception of these, the main sources of irrigation are from bandhs of earthwork placed across the headwaters of small streams. Owing to the undulating nature of the land surface, these are of great value and irrigate considerable areas.

The soil in the valleys is fertile; that on the higher lands is poor, but capable of great development if properly irrigated and manured. The principal crops are autumn and winter rice, maize, millets such as bajra, pulses of which birhi, muga and kulthi are the most important, oilseeds as sarguja, til, and castor. Sugarcane, tobacco, jute, and hemp are grown in small quantities, and their cultivation is on the increase; while country vegetables do well and potatoes, cabbage, cauliflower and other foreign vegetables introduced in recent years have been successful and their cultivation is being gradually extended.

The manufacturing industries of the State are in the main of a primitive nature and provide goods for local consumption only. The chief exception to this is the weaving of tassar cloth which is done on considerable scale in Bahmanghatti and Olmara parganas. The cloth which is manufactured from local cocoons is of good quality and pleasing design and is exported in large quantities for sale, chiefly to the Central Provinces and Madras Presidency.

Coarse and strong cotton cloth is manufactured everywhere for local sale to the aboriginal population. The local blacksmiths are skilful in turning out axes, spades, knives, sickles, etc., of very fair quality; the carpenters in addition to making ordinary household chattels, add to their profits by the manufacture of combs, beads, boxes and other fancy articles; the Domes and Mahalies are expert in the weaving of baskets, boxes, fans, and mats.

The population at the last census numbered 729,400. The great majority live by cultivation, but the aboriginal tribes earn a proportion of their livelihood by labour on earthwork, tree-felling and sawing, and collection of jungle produce, while many emigrate to work on railways, mines, etc., and in harvesting crops in neighbouring districts for some months in each year.

The aboriginal and semi-aboriginal tribes comprise over 70 per cent. of the whole population. The chief are the Santhals and next come the Kols, the Bhumijs and the Kurmis. Of these semi-Hinduized tribes the Bhuinyans, Bathuris, Pans, Gonds, and Khonds are the principal.

The pure Hindu castes form only about 14 per cent. of the population. The most numerous of these are the Gauras, and next come the Khandaits, followed by the Kamars, Kumhars, and Brahmans.

The people in general are very backward in education, which is confined at present chiefly to the Hindu element. The official language of the State and that most commonly used by the majority of the inhabitants is Uriya, but the aboriginal tribes use their own languages as well, of which the most important and widely known is Santhali. The people, on the whole, are truthful, peaceable, and law-abiding. Some of the aboriginal tribes such as the Santhals, Bhuinyans, and Khonds are noted for their fidelity and hospitality. They are frank and honest, and simplicity and honesty characterise most of the wild and unsophisticated races. Every stranger entering a village is offered food and is an honoured guest as long as he remains. But those of the aboriginal tribes who have come in contact with town life and its resulting evils have lost their primitive simplicity and have become shrewd, artful, insincere, and litigious. The favourite drink of the aboriginal tribes is handia or pachwai (rice beer), which they use extensively on festive and ordinary occasions. Both Hindus and aborigines are addicted to opium-eating, more especially on the eastern side of the State.

The climate of the State is fairly healthy, but the hill and jungle tracts are malarious. Malarial fever is the most prevalent disease and accounts for the largest number of deaths. Dysentery is of frequent occurrence: while cholera and small-pox make their appearance in epidemic form at intervals, but thanks to the efficient medical service and preventive measures established by the late Chief, they do not now assume serious proportions.

CHAPTER II.

A Short History of the Raj Family.

Materials for an authentic and detailed history of Mayurbhanj State and its ruling family from its foundation till modern times are non-existent. Brief references are found in some tales of local wars and accounts of travels, but beyond this there is nothing but verbal tradition as preserved in the family to account for its origin and progress. It may be accepted as sufficiently authentic to show that Maharaja Sri Ram Chandra was the descendant of a long line of ancestors of good family, capable and bold in asserting and maintaining their rights and safeguarding their territory but not turbulent or wantonly oppressive, fighting for their own when the need arose, but in general living in peace with their neighbours so long as the latter remained at peace with them.

According to tradition, recorded by Sir William Hunter, Mayurbhanj was founded more than 2,000 years ago, but according to the tradition and chronicles found in possession of the late State Chhamukaran Damodar Pattnaik about 1,300 years ago, by Jai Singh, a relative of the then Maharaja of Jaipur, in Rajputana. Jai Singh came on a pilgrimage to the shrine of Jagannath at Puri and, according to one account, married the daughter of Gajapati, Raja of Puri, and received Hariharpur as dowry; but according to the local tradition he came to Puri with his two sons, Adi Singh and Jati Singh, the elder of whom was married to the daughter of the Raja of Puri.

When returning home Jai Singh overthrew a chieftain named Mayurdhwaja, then holding the gadi of Bahmanghatti, and assumed the title of "Bhanj," meaning "Breaker," which accounts for the present name of the State. Bahmanghatti is regarded ever since that date as the original place of residence of the Raj family. In every State seal the design of a peacock was introduced as a family distinction. It is a curious fact that the peacock is also a heraldic bird of Rajputana, where, as well as in Mayurbhanj, the killing of the sacred bird is prohibited. This may be merely a coincidence, or it may be corroborative evidence of the Rajput origin of the Mayurbhanj Chiefs.

Jai Singh settled in Mayurbhanj and ruled there from 598 to 618 A.D. He divided the territory of Hariharpur, which comprised both Mayurbhanj and Keonjhar, between his two sons. Adi Singh, the elder, got Mayurbhanj and built his fort at Adipur, while Jati Singh got Keonjhar and made his headquarters at Jatipur, on the opposite bank of the Baitarni. Adi Bhanj succeeded his father and ruled from 618 to 656. He divided his territory into 22 provinces and appointed over each a Sarbarakar, whose duty it was to support his Chief in war and to realize the revenue, half of which he paid to the Chief and half he retained as his own reward. The office of Sarbarakar was hereditary on condition of continued loyalty and obedience.

Adi Bhanj was followed by his son, Nilambar Bhanj, who died in 689. Nilambar Bhanj had two sons, Kishore Bhanj and Laksman Raj Bhanj, but the elder brother being absent on a pilgrimage at the time of his father's death the younger was placed on the gadi. Kishore Bhanj on his return accepted the situation and was provided with certain territory for his maintenance. His descendants hold some revenue-free villages in Pargana Adipur to this day.

During the administration of Laksman Raj Bhanj, the Sarbarakar of Joshipur (formerly Daspur) rebelled and was defeated in a fight in which many aboriginal soldiers were killed on both sides.

Laksman Raj Bhanj was succeeded in 726 by his eldest son, Biseswar Bhanj. His second son, Jagadiswar Bhanj, by dint of cleverness and intelligence, became the Raja of Kanika, in Cuttack district. Biseswar Bhanj turning an oppressor, the subjects, with the help of several Sarbarakars, broke out in rebellion. Biseswar Bhanj, with the help of Raja Ananta Bhanj of Keonjhar, quelled the rebellion, beheaded the rebellious Sarbarakars, and appointed new ones in their place. The Sarbarakars of Simlipal, Bahmangatti, and Joshipur remained faithful to their Chief during this rebellion and were, therefore, liberally rewarded. After Biseswar Bhanj his only son, Bharat Bhanj, ruled from 764 to 804. He was a very good and pious Chief, who took particular interest in the welfare of his subjects. He was so very religious that he would not take any food without performing the due religious rites and reading the sacred Shastras every day. He freely gave charity to the poor and the distressed, so much so that the balance in his treasury never reached a thousand rupees. During his rule the people lived in perfect peace and happiness. He had two sons, the elder of whom, Dilipeswar Bhanj, succeeded his father. He was an able administrator and the people lived in peace under him, no one daring to do harm to his neighbour. But, unlike his father, instead of spending his money for the public good, he stored his treasury with valuable things. His younger brother, Madhusudan, while out on a hunting excursion, was killed by a tiger. Dilipeswar Bhanj was succeeded by his son, Bamandev Bhanj, in 839. He was very intelligent and physically strong too. He died in 878 and was followed by his son, Basudev, who ruled till 916. Basudev had two sons, Keshari Bhanj and Harihar Bhanj. The former succeeded his father, and the latter became Raja of Keonjhar, as the then Raja, Santai Bhanj, had no son. Keshari's son and successor, Narayan Bhanj (960—996), has the reputation of having been cruel and oppressive. His son, Nilkantha Bhanj, followed him and was in turn succeeded, in 1028, by his son, Birkeswar Bhanj, who was fond of learning. Birkeswar's eldest son, Kapileswar, followed him on the gadi in 1064 and expelled his three younger brothers from the State on learning that they were plotting against him. On his death in 1100, he was succeeded by his son, Trilochan, who ruled till 1138. Trilochan's eldest son, Rajkishore Shan, had died before his father, who was therefore succeeded by his youngest son, Dasarthi Bhanj (1138—1164). He is reputed to have been wise and intelligent but severe withal. He dismissed and punished several Sarbarakars for disobedience, and in the course of his pursuit of them he removed his headquarters from Adipur, which had hitherto been the capital, and built garhs successively at Simlipal, Kainsari, and Karkachia. He was followed by his son, Srikrishna, who built the Khuradia Garh, and dealt even-handed justice to all and treated all people with equal consideration till his death in 1195. Srikrishna was succeeded by his son, Gadadhar, who died in 1236, and his son, Aruneswar Bhanj, ruled in turn till 1264. He imposed heavy taxes on the people, and built the temples of Kinchakeswari and Siva at Adipur. These temples still exist and contain many carvings and statues of considerable antiquarian and religious interest. Aruneswar Bhanj was succeeded by his son, Gopinath Bhanj, who was followed in 1279 by his son, Radhakrishna Bhanj, who in his turn gave place to Prithwinath Bhanj in 1301. As Prithwinath Bhanj had no son, he adopted Baikuntha Bhanj, the youngest son of Raja Trilochan Bhanj of Keonjhar, who succeeded his adoptive father and ruled from 1334 to 1360. This is the first break in the direct line of descent, a member of the collateral branch becoming the Chief of Mayurbhanj.

Baikuntha Bhanj had four sons, the eldest of whom was killed by his brothers, of whom the youngest, Bireswar, was elected Raja. Bireswar was of a religious turn of mind and built the Rahani Garh and the temple of Siva at Khuradia. As he had no son, he adopted Ram Chandra Bhanj, the son of his second brother, who ruled from 1390 to 1423. He built a garh and a temple of Siva at Mantri. A grand annual fair is still held at Mantri on the day of the Sivaratri, and the temple built by him still exists. Part of the jungle *mahal* adjoining Midnapur was attacked by him and added to his territories under the name of Bhanja-bhumi. His elder son, Balabhadra Bhanj, succeeded him in 1423 and reigned till 1464. He consulted his younger brother, Narayan Bhanj, in all matters. He excavated a big tank at Amarda, which remains unique in size and purity to this day. As the Sarbarakar of Nilgiri died without a son, he appointed his own son by his second wife Raja of Nilgiri and entrusted him with the charge of Kainsari, Kaptipada, and Nilgiri. Balabhadra was succeeded in 1464 by Harekrishna Bhanj, his son by his first wife, who built a garh and several temples at Hariharpur. The ruins of these still exist and are noted for their curious and elaborate brick carvings and traceries, many of which are still in a good state of preservation. His son, Nilkantha Bhanj, succeeded him in 1491 and was in turn followed in 1520 by his son, Santhai Bhanj. Santhai Bhanj made over Bhanja-bhumi to the Raja of Midnapur. He was an able administrator and well versed in arms. The big tank at Baripada and the Baghsamal Garh owe their origin to him. He had two sons, Baidynath Bhanj and Jagadiswar Bhanj, and was succeeded by the former in 1556. Baidynath Bhanj was converted to the worship of Vishnu and the temples of Haribalava Dev Mahaprabhu, Natmandir, and Goondichamandir at Baripada are monuments to his fame and piety. The people lived in safety, peace and happiness during his administration. He was succeeded by his son, Jagannath Bhanj, in 1600, who attacked the pargana of Khelar belonging to the Zamindar of Nayagram, in Midnapur, but as the latter, appearing before him, acknowledged submission in a respectful manner, Jagannath Bhanj was pleased with him and made over the pargana to him. He was a wise and experienced administrator, always eager to promote the welfare of his people, and so after his death he was deeply mourned by all his subjects. He was succeeded by his son, Harihar Bhanj, in 1643, who was noted for his severity. During his rule the punishment for theft was death. He died in 1688, and was succeeded by his son, Sarbeswar, who was in turn followed in 1711 by his son, Bikramaditya Bhanj. As the Raja of Nilgiri died without any issue, Bikramaditya made his youngest brother's son, Dasarath, the Raja of Nilgiri.

About this period we find one of the few references to Mayurbhanj in contemporary Indian history. In the "Riyāz-us-Sālātin" of Ghulam Hussain Salim, it is recorded that when Ali Verdi Khan was marching against Murshid Quli Khan in Orissa in 1741, he was opposed at Rajghat on the Subarnarekha river by Raja Jagardhar Bhanj of Mayurbhanj. Ali Verdi Khan asked help of the Raja, which was refused, whereupon he bombarded the Raja's entrenchments from the opposite bank of the river and the Raja and his forces were compelled to withdraw. Ali Verdi Khan crossed the river and met and defeated Murshid Quli Khan near Balasore, and after settling Orissa returned to Bengal. The Governor of Orissa, whom he had appointed, was shortly afterwards ousted by Mirza

Baqir, son-in-law of Murshid Quli Khan, and Ali Verdi Khan had again to march on Orissa in 1742, where he defeated and expelled the usurper. The "Riyāz-us-Sālātin" then goes on to relate that as Jagat Isar, Raja of Mayurbhanj, apparently the same Raja as the historian names Jagardhar before, had taken sides with Mirza Baqir. Ali Verdi Khan, after subduing the latter, came back to Balasore and set about punishing the Raja, who was then at his palace at Hariharpur. The Raja, relying on his forces, resisted, but was at length compelled to flee "to the top of a hill and hide himself in a secret fastness beyond the ken of discovery. Ali Verdi Khan then subjugated the tract of Mayurbhanj, showed no quarter, and mercilessly carried fire and sword through its limits."

The "Seir Mutaqherin" gives a somewhat different account of these events. In it we find that "the Raja of Mayurbhanj had exceedingly harassed the army proceeding to Orissa, being under personal attachment to Mirza-Baqir." The Viceroy Ali Verdi Khan therefore destined him to punishment. When Ali Verdi was returning victorious from Orissa "the Raja threw himself into the arms of Mustapa Khan (Ali Verdi's Afghan General) who interceded vigorously for him. This intercession had no effect in softening Ali Verdi. The Raja, however, relying apparently on the power of Mustapha Khan to protect him, presented himself at the camp without a safe conduct, and he and all his suite were incontinently put to death, by Mir-jaafer Khan, and his country was thereafter plundered and sacked. Mustapha Khan naturally considered this a great affront and dishonour to himself. Scarcely was the invasion of Mayurbhanj finished when the Mahrattas appeared in Bengal, and Ali Verdi Khan hurrying to meet them was surrounded and in danger of destruction. Mustapha Khan and his Afghan colleagues displayed a mutinous spirit and showed no energy in repelling the Mahrattas; and this incident of the murder of the Raja of Mayurbhanj was put forward as one of their principal grievances. Ali Verdi Khan, however, threw himself on the magnanimity of his General and won him over.

Though this narrative shows that the Raja of Mayurbhanj took a part in struggles of that time in Orissa, there is no mention of those events in the family traditions. These state that the Raja of that time was one Raghunath Bhanj, who ruled from 1728 to 1750, and having no heir adopted Chakradhar Bhanj, the second son of the Raja of Keonjhar, who ruled till 1761. But the account in the "Seir Mutaqherin" is probably accurate, the historian being a contemporary and a friend of Ali Verdi's family; and it seems probable that the adoption of Chakradhar Bhanj from the collateral branch of the family in Keonjhar was necessitated by the fact that the Raja with his heirs, if he had any, perished as described at the hands of Ali Verdi Khan.

Chakradhar Bhanj was succeeded by his son, Damodar Bhanj, who had two wives—Sumitra Devi and Jamuna Devi—but no son. At the time of his death he nominated Tribikram Dev, son of Balbhadra Bhanj, Raja of Keonjhar, as his heir ; but his wives, instead of carrying out his instructions, ruled themselves. The officers of the State tried to make over the administration to Tribikram, but did not succeed. Rani Sumitra Devi Bhanj ruled from 1796 to 1805, and was followed by the second Rani, who ruled for some years and was then succeeded by Tribikram Bhanj.

In 1782, during the rule of Damodar Bhanj, we find the first reference to Mayurbhanj State in British records. In 1784 the Raja voluntarily agreed to pay a tribute of £320 a year to the British Government, which sum was reduced in 1812. Sir William Hunter notes that from that time, till our expulsion of the Mahrattas in 1803, the State seems to have remained in "a chronic condition of invasion, insurrection, and internecine feud. Since our accession foreign invasion has ceased, and seven years later we put a stop to internal commotions by definitely recognizing one of the claimants as Raja, and supporting him in his office with a high hand." The rule of the two Ranis appears, therefore, to have been a very disturbed one, and it is probable that they only held it as against rival claimants by virtue of their right of possession. The State came under British control with the conquest of Orissa in 1803, prior to which it had been feudatory to the Mahrattas; but owing to there being no definitely recognized Chief, no treaty was concluded with it in 1803 or 1804, as was done with the other States of Orissa, and it was, therefore, not included in the list of States mentioned in section 36 of Regulation XII of 1805. After Tribikram Bhanj was finally recognized as Raja in 1810, a treaty was concluded with him in 1812, in which the tribute of the State was fixed at Rs. 1,001, and the Raja agreed, amongst other things, to forego his claim to levy a tax on pilgrims who had to pass through the State on their journey to and from Jagannath. Tribikram Bhanj executed a second ekrarnama in 1815.

Tribikram Bhanj died in 1822 and was succeeded by his son, Jadhunath Bhanj, who entered into a treaty engagement with the British Government in 1829, binding himself over to maintain himself in submission and loyalty to the East India Company's service, and for himself, his heirs, and successors, to pay annually in perpetuity as peshkash sicca Rs. 1,001 to that Government, and, after providing for the extradition of offenders and the passage of the troops of the East India Company through his territories, further engaged himself, in the event of any neighbouring Raja or other person offering opposition to the East India Company's government, to depute a contingent of his own troops to act in concert with those of the Company to coerce and bring such Raja or other person into subjection.

Jadhunath Bhanj was an able and enlightened ruler for his time. He was kind, charitable, and devoted to the welfare of his subjects and was in the good graces of Government. He dismissed several Sarbarakars for their acts of injustice and oppression and appointed his own Tahsildars in their places. The Sarbarakar of Bahmanghatti, Narendra Mahapatra, created a disturbance which was put down with some difficulty, and Bahmanghatti was taken under the direct control of the Chief. Only the Sarbarakar of Kaptipada was allowed to retain his office, and his successors do so to this day, though they have frequently proved refractory subjects, asserting a quasi-independence even in the time of Maharaja Sri Ram Chandra, to whom the then Sarbarakar gave much trouble.

Jadunath Bhanj was succeeded by his son, Srinath Bhanj, in 1863, but as, in order to understand and appreciate the share which Maharaja Sri Ram Chandra had in developing the State of Mayurbhanj, and the foundation on which he had to work, a short but rather more detailed account of its administration under Srinath Chandra and his successor Krishna Chandra appears necessary, this may more conveniently form the subject of a separate chapter.

CHAPTER III.

MAYURBHANJ UNDER SRINATH CHANDRA BHANJ DEO AND KRISHNA CHANDRA BHANJ DEO.

JADUNATH BHANJ had three sons, Srinath Bhanj, Sitanath Bhanj, and Dwarka Nath Bhanj. The eldest son, Srinath Bhanj, succeeded him, but failed to carry on the efficient and just policy of his father. Though simple and kind-hearted, he was also weak, luxurious, and fond of pleasure, and easily led astray by the unscrupulous hangers-on with whom he surrounded himself. He lived for pleasure and neglected the affairs of the State; when he did interfere in them his actions, undertaken on the advice of his unscrupulous followers, were most arbitrary with the natural result that the administration was disorganized and his authority was set at defiance. The people of Bahmanghatti and Upperbhag took to rioting and looting, in consequence of which the subdivision of Bahmanghatti was taken under the direct control of Government in 1866, and its management was made over to the Deputy Commissioner of Singbhum; and further, a police-station was opened by Government at Bankati in the Upperbhag pargana to keep the people of that area in order.

He had no children of his own, and his heir was, therefore, Krishna Chandra Bhanj, the eldest son of his younger brother. Srinath Chandra, however, hated the children of this brother and did his best to disinherit Krishna Chandra and to appoint an orphan Brahmin boy as his successor. Fortunately for the State, and for Krishna Chandra, he had a powerful friend in Mr. T. E. Ravenshaw, the then Commissioner of the Orissa Division and Superintendent of the Tributary Mahals, who opposed Srinath Chandra's attempt to disinherit his nephew, and appointed the latter as Manager of the State. The Raja, however, cared nothing for his advice and continued his vicious life, doing all that he could to interfere with his nephew's attempts to bring order into the administration of the State.

Srinath Chandra died in 1868 and was succeeded by Krishna Chandra Bhanj, who at once began gradually to put into effect the reforms in administration which he had vainly attempted to inaugurate during his uncle's life-time. He was only eighteen years of age at the time of his succession, and was a handsome and intelligent young man, of ready resource and charming manners. He had no English education, but proved himself a very able and wise ruler, and was assisted and advised in his work by Mr. Ravenshaw, who had a high regard for him. He had no easy time at first, as the intrigues against him, begun under the rule of Srinath Chandra, were continued after the latter's death by some of his officers, who tried to deprive him of hisl egal right to the Gadi. The widowed Rani of Srinath Chandra too, for some time, helped these designing persons, but without success. When she realised that an attempt to disinherit Krishna Chandra would not be just or fair and was sure to prove abortive, she gave up the idea and began to show favour to him. It required no small amount of tact and wisdom on the part of young Krishna Chandra to win the favour and affection of his aunt, who had been actively concerned in the plot to ruin him. Fortunately for Mayurbhanj, in Krishna Chandra she found a ruler who, though not a puritan in character, had many good qualities of head and heart. With commendable zeal and earnestness he tried to promote the best interests of the State, planting the tree of progress, which developed and spread its branches under the fostering care of his son, Sri Ram Chandra,—the theme of this book. He was created a Maharaja in 1877 for his efficient administration of the State and for his public liberality, the most prominent instance of which was his donation of Rs. 27,000 towards raising the Cuttack High School to the status of a college—which is now known as the Ravenshaw College—the only college in Orissa ; and in recognition of his able and efficient rule, the subdivision of Bahmanghatti was restored to his direct control in 1878.

Previous to the accession of Krishna Chandra, no attempt had been made to introduce into the State modern methods of administration. Jadunath Bhanj, while a wise and efficient Chief, had merely continued the personal rule of his forefathers with the help of his Diwan and other ancestral officers. Krishna Chandra had to create every department, practically from the beginning. He established civil, criminal, and revenue courts and appointed special officers to their charge, each with a sufficient complement of subordinates. Formerly the administration of justice had not been systematically carried on, there being no books or records or documents of any sort. The Diwan or other officers who were empowered to try particular cases disposed of them verbally after hearing both sides and their witnesses. Paper was very seldom used, such writing as was done being on palm leaves. Except the Diwan, all other officers used to squat on mats or carpets while trying cases or discharging other duties. As a special distinction the Diwan had a quilt on a carpet for his seat with several big pillows for his comfort. The Diwan had nothing to do with writing ; all that he had to do was to pass verbal orders and sign his name where necessary. Maharaja Krishna Chandra abolished this obsolete system and provided all superior officers with tables and chairs, and the ministerial officers with benches. Only the nazirs, moharrirs, and other subordinate officials used carpets as before. Record books relating to cases were ordered to be kept, files were introduced, plaints and written statements, evidence of witnesses and the judgments of the courts were ordered to be written on paper, and the use of the antiquated palm leaves was done away with. A record room for the safe custody of all documents, registers, and papers was established. Process peons were engaged and process fees charged for the service of summons and notices, but court fees were not charged till towards the close of his rule, when they were imposed to a nominal amount. Some mukhtears were allowed to appear for parties in suits, and a State pleader was engaged to conduct cases on behalf of the State. A Registry Office was created at Baripada, and a Sub-Registrar appointed under the Collector for the registration of deeds of sale, mortgage, etc. If any one was dissatisfied with the order of a lower court, he could prefer an appeal to the Chief, who called for the papers, and after having heard the arguments of the mukhtears on both sides, finally disposed of the case, writing the judgments in important cases in the vernacular with his own hand. All people were satisfied with the even-handed justice dealt out by Maharaja Krishna Chandra.

The rudiments of a separate police department were created by the investiture of each Sardar of every pargana in Mayurbhanj proper with police powers. They discharged the duties of a Sub-Inspector of Police in their respective jurisdictions and dealt with petty cases, important cases being personally investigated by some of the higher officers of the State. The Sardars of Panchpir were not invested with police powers, but a police-station was established in that subdivision, at Joshipur, in charge of a Sub-Inspector, under whom there were some constables. Constables were also stationed at Baripada to police the town.

Up to this time there had been no jail in existence. An under-trial prisoner was secured in stocks, which held fast one of his feet in such a manner that escape was impossible. Prisoners were generally fined and seldom sentenced to imprisonment; hence the want of a jail was not seriously felt. If any prisoner was ever sentenced to a term of imprisonment, he was put in the stocks for the period. This form of stocks is still in use in French Chandernagore and is known as torang. Krishna Chandra abolished this form of punishment and built a proper jail and a hajat for under-trial prisoners. Those who underwent civil imprisonment were housed in a separate part of the jail building. A Brahman cook was engaged to cook the prisoners' food. Convicts were made to work in the State gardens, and on the buildings and roads when necessary.

The assessment of land revenue had previously been made in a rough and ready manner, the pradhan or village headman engaging to pay so much to the State and taking for himself all he collected from the raiyats above that amount. In order to put a stop to the malpractices of some unscrupulous pradhans, who used to charge excessive rents from the cultivators by leasing out lands without any measurement and fixing rates at their own sweet will, Survey and Settlement operations were introduced and carried out pargana by pargana. The Uriya system of measurement was employed, and records of the Survey and Settlement prepared and preserved. The State was divided into districts and parganas, and a Sardar was appointed in each pargana. The pradhans collected rent from the cultivators in their respective villages and paid it to their Sardars, who in their turn made over the amounts to the State Treasury. The Sardars and pradhans were remunerated in some cases by a fixed percentage of the total jamas assessed, and in other cases by the proceeds of settlement of all waste lands which might be brought under cultivation within the period of their engagements. If the cultivators witheld payments, the pradhans brought rent suits against them in the Collector's Court, and similarly the Sardars also might sue the pradhans for non-payment of the revenue collection in time, and they themselves in their turn might be sued by the State for the same reason.

A Public Works Department was established under the charge of Mr. J. L. Atkinson, for the erection and repair of State buildings and the construction of roads. There was no system previously for the execution of such work. Such roads as existed were mere tracks; even in the town of Baripada there were no metalled roads. Water accumulated in places in the Sadar road and water-lilies grew there, much to the inconvenience of officers who had occasion to go to the Rajbati. After reaching the Rajbati they had to wash their muddy feet before taking their seats, and for this purpose a pail of water was constantly kept ready in a particular corner. The metalling of this Sadar road was one of the first works of the newly created department, and after this several other pucca roads were created within and without the town. The roads from Baripada to Balasore and from Baripada to Bahalda were first constructed during this administration.

Another important work of this department was the carrying out of additions and alterations to the Rajbati. Formerly, with the exception of the Gol Verandah, Sat Bakhra and one or two buildings in the inner apartment, there were no masonry structures at all; the rest were all thatched huts. These were replaced by brick buildings. The Lion Gate was also built at this time; and other buildings erected such as the school-house, police-station, post-office, jail, a rest-house at Gulapbagh for the reception of Government officials. Some irrigation bandhs were also undertaken, such as that at Mundari in pargana Rasunia.

An Education Department was created, and placed in charge of Dr. H. C. Bowzer, who was also medical officer. A school was established at Baripada and an English-knowing teacher and an Uriya pandit were placed in charge of it. Uriya and elementary English were taught in this school. Several elementary schools were also set up in various places in the Bahmanghatti and Panchpir subdivisions and Uriya abadhans appointed to them. These schools were all free and no fees were charged from the boys, the State bearing all expenses. Later the inspection of the schools was entrusted to Government.

A charitable dispensary was started at Baripada, in charge of Dr. H. C. Bowzer. It was held in a room in the Rajbati. At that time, however, people had no faith in Western medicine, and very few came to Dr. Bowzer for medical help and ultimately he resigned. After some other changes a hospital assistant, Pravakar Das, was placed in charge of the dispensary and succeeded to some extent in making it popular. There was in addition a local native doctor, who dispensed Ayurvedic medicines.

A primitive Postal System was created, by the stationing of a postal clerk at Baripada and another at Balasore. The Baripada clerk sent all letters to the clerk at Balasore, who posted them in the local Government Post Office. The Postmaster at Balasore made over all letters intended for the State to the State clerk at Balasore, who in his turn sent them to the clerk at Baripada for delivery.

Many other miscellaneous institutions had also their origin at this time. Such, for instance, were the printing press at Baripada, where all forms, summonses, warrants, etc., were printed. A newspaper, called the "Mayurbhanj Fortnightly Magazine," was published from that press, the Maharaja bearing all the expenses himself. A Library was established and stocked with a good collection of Bengali and English books. A beautiful garden was laid out at Gulapbagh, where fruits and vegetables of various kinds were grown for the first time.

Such were the rudiments of order and method in administration created by Maharaja Krishna Chandra Bhanj Deo, to replace the primitive rule of his ancestors, and such the foundations on which his son, Sri Ram Chandra, had to build the edifice of State as it now exists. Krishna Chandra was well and faithfully aided by the officers whom he wisely chose to carry out his plans, of whom the most important were his Diwan, Nunda Kumar Mukherji, and, after his death, Diwan Prasanna Kumar Ghosal; Settlement Officer, Babu Durga Prasad Das; Treasury Officer, Babu Artatran

Mahapatra ; and Babu Ramhari Jit Bebarta ; some of whom continued to work under his son. His institutions were continued and improved upon under Government management, in the hands of Mr. H. P. Wylly, who ably and efficiently administered the State during the period of Sri Ram Chandra's minority. But it was left for Sri Ram Chandra to develop and bring into full being these elementary beginnings. He undertook the task with a strong sense of duty and responsibility, and the measure of his success is the measure of that uprightness, conscientiousness, and love of justice which he devoted to the fulfilment of his trust.

CHAPTER IV.

Birth and Early Life of Sri Ram Chandra.

Sri Ram Chandra was born on the 17th December, 1871. The happy event was celebrated with great rejoicing and liberal distribution of alms and money to the poor and to the Brahmans; and in some cases even lands were given by Raja Krishna Chandra to particular individuals. Sri Ram Chandra was ushered into the world with the good wishes of the people and the blessings of God, who reserved some of his choicest favours in store for him.

In his fifth year Sri Ram Chandra was, according to the Hindu custom, initiated into the mysteries of the vernacular alphabet, and received his first lessons from an Uria abadhan. According to the usual practice he had to write on the ground with a piece of chalk. He had a very sharp intellect and retentive memory and never forgot what he was told by his teacher. At times his father expressed great delight at the boy's intelligence and progress, for even at this early period he bade fair to be a great man. This was not to be greatly wondered at, for both his father and his mother were endowed with exceptional intelligence and good sense.

Sri Ram Chandra learned Uriya for about two years from the abadhan. Then a private tutor with some knowledge of English was engaged to give him lessons in English. Along with English, Uriya lessons were also continued as before. After a course of training like this for another two years, he was admitted into the Anglo-Vernacular School at Baripada. Some time afterwards Pandit Govinda Chandra Mahapatra, then a sub-inspector of schools under Government, who was entrusted with the inspection of schools in Mayurbhanj and Keonjhar, was appointed as his private tutor and taught him Sanskrit and laid the foundation of his education in other subjects. The pandit's services were lent to the State, and he was in later years appointed State Collector by his erstwhile pupil, in which post he died in harness.

When he reached the age of nine years, Sri Ram Chandra's Upanayana ceremony was performed amid great rejoicings, and he was invested with the sacred thread which the Kshatriyas, like the Brahmins, are entitled to wear. Thereafter two years rolled on smoothly, and then the boy received a terrible blow, for he lost both his father and his mother within a few days of each other.

The tragic event, swift and merciless in its onslaught, was not without a touch of the sublime. Maharaja Krishna Chandra had a mind to retire on the completion of his son's education, but that was not to be. The terrible scourge of small-pox broke out at Baripada, and Sri Ram Chandra was one of the first to be attacked by the fell disease. He was the apple of his father's eye, and Krishna Chandra's anxiety knew no bounds. He touched no food and took no sleep, but watched night and day by the sick bed of his beloved son. His constant prayer was, "My darling, may you recover, and may your disease take me," and this was fulfilled. More things are wrought by prayer than we know of. Sri Ram Chandra recovered, but Maharaja Krishna Chandra, the Maharani and other members of the Raj family were attacked by the disease, which was then doing terrible havoc in the town. The Civil Surgeon and the Magistrate of Balasore came to Baripada to render all possible aid, but all human efforts to save Krishna Chandra proved futile, and he was cut off in the prime of his life on the 29th of May, 1882, when he was only 34 years old. History records a parallel case which will bear repetition here. When Humayun was lying seriously ill on one occasion, his father, Baber, the founder of the Moghul Empire in India, walked seven times round the sick bed, uttering some prayers from the Koran the while. This done he exclaimed: "I have taken it away, I have taken it away," and it is stated that from that day Humayun began to recover but Baber's health declined, and when the son was restored to health the father passed away.

The whole of Mayurbhanj was plunged into deep sorrow at the untimely death of Maharaja Krishna Chandra, for he was a very popular ruler, gifted with many a good quality of head and of heart. And misfortune did not come singly, for, after a few days, his pious and devoted wife, the Maharani, joined her husband in that blessed region where sorrow and separation are unknown. The terrible shock which Sri Ram Chandra, then a tender boy in his twelfth year, received can better be imagined than described, suddenly deprived as he was of the fostering care and guidance of an affectionate father and the gentle influence of a loving mother. The boy naturally felt stunned by the blow and, being of a shy disposition, he now became exceedingly moody and dejected.

As Sri Ram Chandra was a minor, the State came under the direct control of the Superintendent of the Tributary Mahals of Orissa and Mr. H. P. Wylly was appointed as its Manager, in December 1882. Maharaja Krishna Chandra had left three sons and four daughters. Of these the second son was adopted in 1882 by the childless Raja of Nilgiri, and eventually became the Raja of that State. The third son, Shreedam Chandra Bhanj Deo, then an infant, now lives at Baripada where he is manager of domestic affairs, and, in his keen interest in the education and training of the present minor Chief and the great and good influence of his upright and pious character, supplies as far as is possible the place of the father of whom the youth has been so unhappily deprived. Mr. Wylly wrote of the three brothers in his Annual Report for 1882-83: "The young Raja is a quiet and good-dispositioned boy, who, with different surroundings and influences, could be trained into a good, manly Chief. He appears to me to be delicate. This may be due to want of exercise and good food. The boy, adopted by the Nilgiri Raja, has more life and vitality than his elder brother. He has also a better constitution. The youngest boy is only four years old."

The future training and career of Sri Ram Chandra proved the soundness of this early estimate of his character. He continued his studies at the Baripada School for about a year more, after which the Superintendent of the Orissa Tributary Mahals made arrangements for his further education at Cuttack, whither he was sent in 1884 in charge of Pandit Govinda Mahapatra, much to the distress of his grandmother, who strongly objected to parting with the boy and for about a week refused to return to the Palace quarters. However, she soon perceived the wisdom of the step taken and became reconciled to the separation. She utterly refused, however, to allow the youngest boy to go to Cuttack with his brother as was proposed by the Superintendent.

From this time on Sri Ram Chandra was placed in charge of another man about whom we must here say something in detail, for naturally in the study of a life it is of importance and interest to learn something of the formative influences which have been brought to bear on the character portrait, especially those of the earlier plastic years; so it will not be out of place to introduce one who had the greatest influence on Sri Ram Chandra from his thirteenth year till his death, for both the pupil and his guardian finished their life-tasks within a few months of each other. In the year 1884, Sir Rivers Thomson, the Lieutenant-Governor of Bengal, requested Mr. H. Bartram Kiddell to go up to Darjeeling and see him on important business. Without knowing in the least the nature of the business, Mr. Kiddell on arrival called at The Shrubbery, and was offered the charge of the minor Raja of Mayurbhanj. To his enquiry as to where Mayurbhanj was, the reply was given, "Away in the jungle tracts of Orissa." The guardian-elect, however, was told that for the major part of his time he would have to reside at Cuttack to provide greater facilities for education. Fascinated by the idea of shaping a life which held such potentialities, Mr. Kiddell accepted the charge. Sir Rivers Thomson in his characteristic way demanded from him whether "he would take him as his own son and make a man of him, not a scholar only or a sportsman." The reply, "I will, sir," given in the emphatic manner, so well known to the people of Mayurbhanj, was

Mr. H. B. Kiddell.

faithfully kept through twenty-seven years of stress and strain that would have dismayed a less courageous man.

The route having been ascertained, a passage was taken by steamer to Cuttack, and farewells were said, in a manner that implied, as a friend expressed it: "We thought Kiddell was disappearing from civilization." In those days there was a Hindustani saying which meant "He who goes to Cuttack never returns." On arrival at Cuttack Mr. Kiddell found his charge under the care of Pandit Govinda Chandra Mahapatra, who was thereafter retained by Government as assistant tutor. The English greeting of "Good-evening, sir," with which he was welcomed in the early morning, was often referred to with amusement by the Maharaja in later years when his knowledge of English had improved so much and his accent was so perfect that, on one occasion at least, Royalty complimented him on it. It had been arranged that Mr. Kiddell should occupy a separate house and control the young Raja of Dhenkanal as well as his more particular charge This did not prove satisfactory; so, on the death of the genial young Chief of Dhenkanal, who was a great favourite with all who knew him, Mr. Kiddel obtained permission to take up his residence in the Mayurbhanj House. From that time on for twelve years the Maharaja of Mayurbhanj shared the same roof as his master, this close relationship continuing for six years after the young Chief attained his Gadi. Thus a firm friendship was cemented and a respect for the older man created, which no false slanders and no differences of opinion on matters of administration could eradicate. No single act of disobedience was known to have been committed nor any disrespect of authority ever shown by the young Chief during his minority; yet he was not without spirit, for there were occasional assertions of "rights" over a younger brother in which some muscular prowess was displayed to show that, although of a quiet and peaceable disposition, he was not prepared to knuckle under to the more assertive youngster.

Various amusing incidents of that period can be recalled, such as the first introduction of soap into the ritual of the bath. This useful commodity was at that time tabooed in ordinary Hindu homes, and its use was considered an innovation worthy of being handed up to the Lieutenant-Governor of Bengal as a breach of caste. However, on this subject of caste no one was more particular than the English guardian, who insisted on all that was essential being performed in the usual way. At the same time the Maharaja very quickly learnt from example that the phrase often on the lips of Mr. Kiddell, "Remember a man's a man, though he is of low caste," was a true one, and at no time afterwards did he show contempt for any human being, except on account of contemptible deeds.

As a boy Sri Ram Chandra was very moody and rather shy and reserved. During their morning rides, Mr. Kiddell used to point out to him various things of interest in passing. At first he was annoyed at being disturbed in his meditations, but he afterwards grew keen to forestall his companion in remarking on objects worthy of notice; and great was his triumph when he discovered things missed by his tutor. One of his chief characteristics in after-life was keen and intelligent observation.

Mrs. Kiddell, too, had no small share in forming the character of Sri Ram Chandra. She is a woman of fine culture, strong intellect, and brave heart. Her sympathetic nature was manifested in her whole-hearted devotion to the poor lepers of Mayurbhanj, for whom the Maharaja later on founded an asylum, of which Mrs. Kiddell was the guiding spirit and manager. The force of her commanding personality was often gratefully acknowledged by Mr. Kiddell himself, and the sterling qualities of her head and heart are well known to the people of Mayurbhanj who came into close contact with her.

CHAPTER V.

HIS SCHOOL AND COLLEGE LIFE—HIS ACCESSION TO THE GADI.

As a youth Sri Ram Chandra was quiet-natured, reserved, and of a thoughtful turn of mind. From boyhood he was very studious and, unlike most other boys, was more fond of reading than of play; but his studies were not confined to text-books only. He took special delight in reading books on various subjects of general knowledge, particularly of history and literature. One of his early attempts at English writing was the translation from the Uriya Pattas of an account of the State from its beginning up to the time of his father's decease. His fondness for reading was phenomenal, and no recreation was more enjoyed by him in later years when it took the place of shikar on which he was very keen in his earlier days. Grimm's Fairy Tales he read and re-read, as well as all the usual books of adventure which boys delight in. Rapidly he passed on to John Stuart Mill and Herbert Spencer, and was rather a trying person to his tutors during that period. Once later in life, referring to that time, he wrote of himself as " an arrogant, ignorant youth, thinking I knew everything, while time has found me more conscious than ever that the Blind Force I was so loud in advocating is a Personal Deity who takes an interest in His creatures." One can say, however, that his arrogance was of a much more bearable type than that of many of his companions.

He was fond of games too, though they took a second place after his books, and were of a somewhat more serious and quiet nature than those indulged in by the average boy. At an early stage he used to amuse himself with playing at "Cutcherry." Chessmen, paperweights, and tiles were utilized for the personnel and make-up of the miniature courts. Charges were framed and cases written up, and pigeons, of which he had a splendid collection, were tried and sentenced, and in one case at least the capital punishment was inflicted and duly carried out. Later on, when court cases of a more serious nature claimed his energy, he turned his attention to military matters. He had a large army of a thousand wooden soldiers, about eight inches in height, fitted with metal weapons and several brass cannon, all locally made. The roof of Belgaria Palace was often the scene of a military review in miniature, but only a very select few were ever allowed to witness it.

He was never a keen rider, but with his guardian was much in the saddle and also out of it, as frequent records in Mr. Kiddell's diary show; the good effect of this was made apparent in his power of sticking on in later life ; and he was fond of his ponies as of all animals. The Commissioner of Orissa once forbade certain ponies being used again on account of their eccentric performances in Ravenshaw College porch and other places. The boy was in Darjeeling when the prohibition was forwarded, through His Honour the Lieutenant-Governor of Bengal. On being asked if he really wanted to keep the ponies, the Maharaja said he did and would be very sorry to part with them.

The then Chief Secretary, who was always an admirer of sporting proclivities, told Mr. Kiddell to keep the ponies, and they lived to a good, if not a righteous, old age in Belgaria stables.

At about the same time, in Darjeeling, the Maharaja won a paper-screen race on his good old polo pony, Tom Pinch. Mrs. Kiddell writes : "Some of us can still remember a New Year's day sports at Baripada when he entered for the 'Tilting at the Ring.' When his rider had taken all the rings Tom Pinch took charge and carried off his master at a mad gallop straight back to the stables. The boy kept his seat and his head, and escaped injury by ducking as the pony rushed into his stall."

He did not take part in the school games at Ravenshaw College as his recreation was provided for outside. Riding was his chief exercise, tennis he played fairly, racquets very well indeed. In his young days football was considered *infra dig.* for a

Chief, but he played a mild game at cricket. Billiards he excelled in, but oriental courtesy forbade his playing his best on his own table against invited guests. He played a good game of chess either in the English or in the Indian mode. There were few English boys and girls in Cuttack, but those there were he fraternized with by riding out with them and going to children's parties, sometimes in fancy dress.

He was very fond of shikar, and learned to use a gun at an early age, and for many years shooting was his favourite sport. Great physical courage was always one of his strong characteristics. Travelling by sea to Cuttack in the "Sir John Lawrence" during the voyage just before that in which she foundered with all hands, a terrible cyclone was encountered, but the Maharaja showed the same fearlessness then as often displayed in later life on land.

He loved travel, but rebelled a good deal at the paraphernalia necessary during his minority; but once the journey was over he thoroughly enjoyed Darjeeling. In 1889 he took a trip to Ceylon with his guardian for the sake of his health. The journey was nearly frustrated at the last moment by the desertion of all the servants from the ship at the moment of casting off—most probably instigated thereto by some unscrupulous hanger-on of the Raj family. Fortunately the Brahmin cook was detained and the food difficulty obviated, and fresh servants were engaged at Colombo. The trip was spoiled to some extent owing to the development of an attack of eczema, but the Maharaja visited Kandy and most of the places of interest in the island. His visit had, however, to be curtailed, much to his disappointment, and though the return voyage did much to restore him to health he had to be placed under medical treatment on his arrival at Calcutta. His eyes were affected, and he had to be placed in a darkened room for some days and was forbidden to read, but such was his love of reading that he managed to secrete a book, with the result that the eyes did not improve till the doctor temporarily dilated the pupils so that reading was impossible.

By nature and in his bearing towards others he was quiet and gentle, never losing temper with, or being rude to, any person, however humble, and being ever careful not to hurt the feelings of anyone by word or deed. His high position never made him overbearing or condescending in his manners; on the contrary, all his dealings with his classmates and associates were marked by an unaffected simplicity and freedom, which, however, never degenerated into undue familiarity. Above all, what reflected the greatest credit on him was his successful maintenance of the purity of his character and life. Though living in the midst of temptations, and surrounded by menials and other people of questionable morality who tried their utmost to lead him astray in order to gain their own selfish ends, he came through the ordeal unscathed. Babu Ram Narayan Sarangi, the retired State Collector of Mayurbhanj, an able and trusted servant of the State since the days of Maharaja Krishna Chandra, in a letter to the author writes :—

" Sri Ram Chandra was very quiet and gentle in his childhood. He never used any harsh words to menials or to anyone else. Bad characters are not wanting at most of the Garjat States even now, and the condition of things was worse a quarter of a century ago. After the death of Maharaja Krishna Chandra, the servants of the Rajbati and other bad characters who had access there tried their best to lead their young master astray, but fortunately they did not succeed. Sri Ram Chandra was able to resist all temptations and keep his character pure. His guardian, Mr. Kiddell, too, had no small share in developing his character and intellect. God in His infinite wisdom placed the young Maharaja under the guidance of Mr. Kiddell."

Sri Ram Chandra passed the Entrance Examination of the Calcutta University, as the Matriculation Examination was then called, from the Ravenshaw Collegiate School in the year 1888, and the First Examination in Arts, now called the Intermediate Examination, two years later. He read up to the B.A. Standard, taking up science and mathematics, for which subjects he had a special aptitude, but though he was very anxious to take his B.A. degree before settling down to the serious business of life, this was not permitted by Government in view of the opposition of the 'Raj family and of his long absence from home. On coming of age he had to return to Mayurbhanj to prepare himself for taking up the reins of administration of his State. He arrived in Baripada from Cuttack on attaining his majority on the 1st March, 1890, and was most enthusiastically received by his people. Thereafter, though he continued his studies under Mr. Kiddell and Babu Mohini Mohan Dhar, M.A. B.L., who coached him in science and mathematics, the cares and responsibilities—both State and domestic—which devolved on him interrupted this study; and when he went to Calcutta to sit for the examination, the illness of Mr. Kiddell and an outbreak of cholera among the people who had followed him upset his arrangements and filled his mind with such care and anxiety as to make his success practically impossible, though he only failed to gain the degree by a very narrow margin.

He assumed full control over the State on the 15th August, 1892, and from this time onward, his studies were directed mainly to philosophy and law, of which he acquired a wide and profound knowledge. He particularly admired and studied British law, the fundamental basis of which is equity and justice,

Belgoria Palace.

and gradually introduced it into his territory thus adopting the form of administration which obtains in British India. In this perhaps he was ahead of his time, but this was the natural outcome of his being far ahead of his people not only in education and culture, but also in power and originality of intellect and ideas.

CHAPTER VI.

SRI RAM CHANDRA'S MARRIAGE—BIRTH OF HIS CHILDREN—DEATH OF HIS WIFE.

A BIOGRAPHER has no right to tread forbidden grounds, but he is in duty bound to record faithfully those facts which had a considerable influence on the life and character of his subject. Hence we shall briefly touch on the events of this chapter without comment or criticism, as they not only aroused a great deal of opposition and bitter feeling at the time of their occurrence, but affected the course of the life both of the Maharaja and of other persons still alive.

When Sri Ram Chandra was a minor of 18 years of age a proposal was made for his marriage with the accomplished third daughter of the late Keshab Chandra Sen, a leader of the Brahmo community in Bengal. He had met and fallen in love with the lady at Darjeeling, and the proposal had his approval as well as that of Mr. Kiddell, his tutor and guardian. The Maharaja, following the bent of his inclination, made up his mind to marry her and with that object in view came up to Darjeeling to settle matters. The engagement though not officially sanctioned, had lasted privately for a few years. But on the grounds of racial, religion and caste differences, such an inter-marriage was strongly opposed, not only by the members of the Raj family, but by the people of Mayurbhanj. In deference to the wishes of his people, and the advice of some high Government officials who were appealed to, Sri Ram Chandra had to give up the idea of that marriage. The renunciation cost him very dear, as the intensity and ardour of a young man's first love, if disappointed, crushes his heart and leaves a lifelong wound which may heal, but a permanent scar remains.' He was ultimately married in 1896 at the age of 25 years to Laksmi Kumari Devi, grand-daughter of Maharaja Nilmani Singh of Chota-Nagpur. The marriage was celebrated with due pomp and jubilation. Maharani Laksmi Kumari Devi was sixteen years old at the time of her marriage. In addition to being a paragon of beauty, she was also an ideal of womanhood, and in a short time not only won the affection of her husband, but commanded the love and regard of all by virtue of her sweet temper, gentle nature, benevolent disposition, graceful manners, and above all her sympathetic heart. Though she was not the "village maiden" of Tennyson's poem, "The Lord of Burleigh," but the grand-daughter of a Maharaja, yet there is a close and pathetic resemblance between her and the lady of the poem, and the following lines mignt well have been written of her:—

> " Shaped her heart with woman's meekness
> " To all duties of her rank :
> " And a gentle consort made she,
> " And her gentle mind was such
> " That she grew a noble lady,
> " And the people loved her much.
>
> * * * * * *
>
> " Three fair children first she bore him,
> " Then before her time she died."

The marriage proved a very happy one but, alas, like all earthly happiness, it was very shortlived, for the last two lines of the poem above quoted were literally fulfilled. The first issue of the marriage was a daughter, who was fair and lovely as a flower and delighted the hearts of all. She was born in 1897. Two years later Tikait Purno Chandra, the present Maharaja, was born, on the 7th August, 1899, and that happy event was celebrated according to family tradition with the customary rites attendant on the birth of an heir amidst great popular rejoicings. Chota Rai Pratap Chandra, the second son, was born in the year 1902. He was very sickly and delicate, and in one sense very unfortunate too for while yet an infant he lost his dear mother on the 6th of March, 1902. She fell a victim to small-pox, a disease which has been fatal to so many of the Raj family of Mayurbhanj and which had carried off Maharaja Krishna Chandra and his wife before. The shock of her death almost crushed Maharaja

Sri Ram Chandra and he was long in recovering from its effects. He renounced all comforts and, though he was a capital sportsman, he gave up all sports from this time and led the life almost of a recluse, abstaining from meat and other delicacies of the table and living only on the most simple fare.

To commemorate the sad and sacred memory of the Maharani, the Laksmi Kumari Dharmsala was founded in 1906. It is a fine and commodious building and affords shelter to all travellers and strangers to Baripada. A beautiful garden was laid out and named Ranibagh in her honour and in it was erected a marble memorial cross whereon are engraved the following inscriptions.

IN LOVING MEMORY

OF

RANI SRIMATI LAKSMI KUMARI DEVI

OF

MAYURBHANJ.

BORN—*25th August*, 1879.

DIED—*6th March*, 1902.

If thou shouldst ask me to resign,
    What most I prize it ne'er was mine—
I only yield thee what is thine,
    Thy will be done.

(*English Translation of the Bengali inscription.*)

Thou passest from the mists and shows of earth,
    It's woes and darkness, to th' eternal clime
Where neither death nor mortal weakness comes, but mirtb
    Breaks in a living stream undried by time.

Thou passest into bright eternity,
    The sunlit courts of Heaven, and the side
Of the immortal gods, who welcome thee
    To where the pure and faithful do abide.

Maharani Lakshmi Kumari Devi Memorial, Ranibag.

CHAPTER VII.

Bestowal of the Title of "Maharaja" on Sri Ram Chandra—His Second Marriage.

As already stated, the young Chief, after attaining his majority, returned to Baripada in 1890 and was given full control of the State in 1892. From that time he devoted himself earnestly and ably to the management of the affairs of his State and in the course of ten years he proved his ability and worth in such a prominent manner that the British Government, which is never slow to recognize and appreciate real merit, conferred on him the title of Maharaja in 1903; for though by courtesy he used to be called Maharaja by the people, the title was not formally bestowed on him by Government until the occasion of the Coronation ceremony of the King-Emperor, Edward VII, in March, 1903. Sir James A. Bourdillon, the officiating Lieutenant-Governor of Bengal, while handing over the Sanad of Maharaja and a Khil'at to the Chief on his investiture at Belvedere, addressed him in the following appreciative words, which are worth quoting as showing the regard in which he was held by Government :—

" Often, before I had the opportunity of making your acquaintance, did the late Lieutenant-Governor speak to me about you in terms of high appreciation and nothing would have pleased him better than himself to have invested you with the title by which I now address you. I am glad to know that you worthily play the rôle of the leading Chief in the Garjat States of Orissa, and that not only in public but in private life you set an admirable example which your fellow Chiefs would do well to follow. The Government are proud to have had during your minority so apt and satisfactory a pupil under their charge. Since you have assumed the control of the Mayurbhanj State you have ruled it wisely and well, while the liberality, which you have shown beyond its borders, has been generous and enlightened. Your father was created Maharaja at the Delhi Assemblage of 1877, and it is a sincere gratification to myself and to your many well-wishers, that the same title was bestowed upon you upon a similar but more splendid occasion. May you long live to enjoy it."

For nearly three years after the death of the Maharani, the Maharaja did not marry again. All this while he bowed to the inevitable and inscrutable decree of fate, but failed to understand why he was subjected to such severe trials, which lacerated his heart and shattered all his dreams of happiness. He felt the loss of his beloved consort very keenly, and he shed many a tear of agony for her in silence and in solitude. Bitter sorrow awakened in him another feeling too—a feeling that he had done an injustice to the lady who had first won his heart and to whom he had pledged his word. Her faithful devotion and constancy to him will read like a romance. She was young, beautiful, and accomplished, but rejected all offers of marriage even from some high quarters. After the marriage of the Maharaja with Laksmi Kumari Devi, for nearly fourteen years she worshipped the idol of her heart in patient silence. Her devoted constancy moved the heart of the Maharaja, and he felt it his duty to do her reparation. But then there were many obstacles of a serious nature in the way. The same difficulties existed as before. On one side was the strong opposition of the people of Mayurbhanj on the grounds of race, religion, and social status ; on the other, the objection of the Brahmo leaders who would not approve of such a marriage unless the Maharaja was converted to Brahmoism. Then again there was the legal aspect of the question, whether the marriage would be valid or not. As the subject has provoked so much speculation and criticism, the following extract from a letter, written before the marriage by the Maharaja to the Dewan Babu Mohini Mohan Dhar in vindication of his own conduct, is quoted as it gives a clear expression of the nature of his motives in the matter and of the doubts and difficulties which he found in the way of obtaining a solution :—

" I thank God that I have gained strength and the opposition is not so acute as it might have been.

I have justice and a sense of duty on my side. I can quite appreciate the people's feeling, but situated as I am in a maze of difficulties what can be the solution? There are moral obligations and the dictates of the inner man on one side, and public feeling and opposition on the other. Must moral principles be respected or policy? Loss of public respect or affection is a big sacrifice, but is it not a virtue in this case? I would fain have preferred a more peaceful life, but I have no control over my circumstances. Fate would have it otherwise. Of course I would not do anything without letting my own people know about it, and if possible bringing them to my view. If they would not approve, they may at least tolerate and appreciate my motives. Of course it would be to my interest, and it would be my duty too, to bring the public to my way of thinking, but I do not know how far that would be possible. This is how matters stand and I have also given you my views. I should like to know your opinion and views, as I have a greater respect for them than for those of any other man in Baripada or elsewhere."

In another letter written to the Dewan after the marriage had taken place, he says :—

" I know there is nothing to be feared from the steps I have taken, yet the feeling of responsibility makes me uneasy. I never aspired to the approval of the populace in the matter which I have taken in hand. I only asked for their toleration and this, I think, is very near being achieved. I can quite understand their feelings, for, had I myself been placed in their position, I would have acted as they have done, if not much worse. I think it is because I could understand and appreciate their feelings and motives that my uneasiness was more acute than it otherwise would have been."

The above quotations need no comment. They express the heart of the man. The Maharaja felt that " justice and a sense of duty " were on his side. He also felt that the opposition of the people was natural and in accordance with their principles and sentiments and that had he been placed in their position and held their views he would have acted like them, if not much worse. He was also conscious that he ran a great risk of losing public respect and affection, which he considered a great sacrifice. It was a trial in which conflicting interests waged war with one another. In the end he gave the preference to " moral principles " over " policy " and made the " big sacrifice," for it must be admitted that the people were never thoroughly reconciled to this marriage, which took place in Calcutta in the year 1904.

CHAPTER VIII.

VISIT OF SIR ANDREW FRASER—OPENING OF THE MAYURBHANJ STATE LIGHT RAILWAY.

THE 2nd December, 1904, was a red-letter day in the annals of Mayurbhanj; for on that day Sir Andrew Fraser, the then Lieutenant-Governor of Bengal, accompanied by Lady Fraser and members of his staff and by Mr. G. F. Growse, the Commissioner of the Orissa Division, and Mr. T. R. Wynne, Agent and Chief Engineer of the Bengal-Nagpur Railway, visited Baripada to perform the opening ceremony of the Mayurbhanj State Light Railway. The occasion was an unique one, not only on account of the completion of the most important and costly public work yet undertaken by the Maharaja, of which we shall make further mention later, but also because no other Lieutenant-Governor had ever visited the State before; and Mayurbhanj did not fail to rise to the honour of the occasion in paying due respect to the ruler of the Province. The decorations and illuminations reflected much credit on those who were responsible for the work and the whole town wore a gay and smiling aspect. When the train reached Baripada at 10 A.M. the Maharaja requested His Honour to declare the railway open and read an address, the main points of which were as follows :—

" It was in 1900-01 that we proposed to construct a light railway of 2 ft. 6 in. gauge to give our people easy access to the Bengal-Nagpur Railway, as well as to develop a promising part of the State, and with this object surveys were made and detailed plans and estimates prepared and submitted to Government at the close of that year. It was not, however, till the close of 1902-03 that sanction was received to the scheme, and actual work did not begin till 1903. . . . . This railway line has been financed entirely from the current revenues of the State and its estimated cost is Rs. 6,00,000 for 32 miles and the expenditure to date has been a little over Rs. 5,75,000. It is expected that the estimate will not be exceeded. . . . .

Placing the working expenses at Rs. 1,300 per mile or Rs. 41,600, in all, the nett profit we arrive at is Rs. 21,180, which gives a return of 3.45 per cent. This is all we expect for the present, but improved communication will no doubt increase the trade in timber and forest products, in which the State is extremely rich and tend also to a general improvement in trade under all heads. Even if the receipts barely meet the working expenses for the time, we shall be satisfied, for our object is not so much to make a profit from the Railway as to afford facility for the development of the resources of the State. . . .

The survey, planning, and execution of the line have lain solely in the hands of Mr. Arnold Martin, State Engineer, who has carried out the construction with the help of the Subordinate Staff of the Public Works Department of the State and the assistance of Messrs. Balmer, Lawrie & Co., Messrs. Martin & Co., and Messrs. Orenstein and Koppel, who together supplied most of the European materials, and of Messrs. Hemchand and Dharsi, General Contractors of Rajkote, Kathiawar, who undertook almost the entire work on the line and executed it with commendable promptness and despatch. To them all my thanks are due."

In declaring the line open His Honour delivered an appreciative speech, from which we quote the following extracts :—

"It is a great pleasure to me to come here to-day and to take part in this pleasant function. I congratulate the Mayurbhanj State on having for its ruler a man like the Maharaja who is determined not to give his days to selfish indulgence, but to devote his energies to the opening up and development of his State and the advancement of its interests. Fortunate indeed it is for the State to have such a ruler. . . .

I believe that there is before the State, under its present enlightened ruler, a period of great development and prosperity: I hope that the Maharaja will be led wisely as well as energetically

Rajbati.

to use the opportunities which he has. There is no one that desires more earnestly than I that he may be long spared to rule the State, and that he may be successful in advancing its interests and happy in the work of administration."

On the afternoon of the same day His Honour presided at the prize-giving of the Baripada High English School, and on the next day Lady Fraser laid the foundation-stone of the Girls' School, and in order to signalise these memorable events the Hostel attached to the High English School was called "Fraser Hostel" and the Girls' School was named the "Lady Fraser Girls' School."

On the evening of the 2nd December the distinguished visitors were entertained at an evening party at the Rajbati, which was also attended by the Raja of Nilgiri, the Raja of Kanika, Raja Baikuntha Nath De of Balasore, besides the elite of the town and the State officials. In proposing the toast to His Honour and Lady Fraser on that occasion, the Maharaja delivered the following speech, which is worth quoting as indicative of his firm loyalty to the Sovereign and his sense of obligation to the British Government:—

"YOUR HONOUR, LADIES AND GENTLEMEN,

It is now my pleasant task to propose a toast which I am sure you will receive with cordiality and enthusiasm. But before I do so, I may be permitted to express the pleasure and pride which I feel at having this opportunity of entertaining Your Honour and Lady Fraser, and of expressing to you, Sir, the loyalty and esteem which I entertain for the British Government.

Loyalty to the Sovereign is a religious injunction in this country and this sentiment finds a prominent place in all well-balanced Indian hearts—all the more because of the many blessings which British rule has conferred on this country. In my own case, I may say that the sentiment of loyalty which is common to all is strengthened by the sense of gratitude for the many benefits which I have received personally from the British Government. After the death of my late lamented father, the care of my person and of my education rested entirely in the hands of Government, and I am eminently thankful for the personal care and attention which it then bestowed on me. Again, during my minority, the State was under Government management and the improvements and progress, which were then started, have served as guides to me for making further improvements and progress. Then, again, in my work of administering the State, I have invariably obtained valuable advice and co-operation from successive Superintendents of Tributary Mahals, and also from Your Honour's Government, and it is to this fact that any success that I have been able to achieve is partly due. Your Honour, these are the reasons why I had always entertained a desire to welcome the Governor of the Province to my capital and there to express to him, as representative of the Sovereign, the obligations under which I lay to his Government. That desire is now fulfilled. I am neither an orator nor even a good speaker ; it would not, therefore, do for me to prolong my speech so as to express in adequate terms my feelings. Gentlemen, I give you the health of my honoured guests, Sir Andrew and Lady Fraser. "

CHAPTER IX.

Death of the Maharaja's Daughter—His Robust Optimism.

Sripad Manjari, the only daughter of the Maharaja, was as intelligent as lovely, and dear to all. Though a girl of only 7 or 8 summers she could speak English fluently and with faultless accent, and on the occasion of the prize-giving presided over by Sir Andrew Fraser at the High School, she recited an English poem in a style so perfect as to surprise all and to elicit the unstinted admiration and applause of His Honour and the other distinguished visitors.

But who suspected that she would be called away so soon? In March 1906, she was attacked with typhoid fever, and though the best medical help available was at once requisitioned from Calcutta and for a time she rallied, she had a relapse and it baffled all human efforts to save her. The delicate flower faded and drooped and on the 9th April, 1906, joined her dear mother in that blessed region where sorrow and death are unknown. Her sad and untimely death naturally calls to mind the lines addressed to "Blossoms" by the poet, which may be most appropriately applied to her :—

> Fair pledges of a fruitful tree,
> Why do ye fall so fast ?
> Your date is not so past,
> But you may stay yet here awhile
> To blush and gently smile
> And go at last.
>
> What were ye born to be
> An hour or half's delight
> And so to bid goodnight ?
> 'Twas pity Nature brought ye forth
> Merely to show your worth
> And lose you quite.

The child was very dear to the Maharaja and the shock of her death affected him very keenly. As he gave his beloved daughter a last farewell kiss at the moment of her death, he fell into a dead faint under the stress of his grief. But shortly afterwards he recovered, and restraining his emotion, he came out to his office room and with tearful eyes signed a cheque for the doctors who had been summoned from Calcutta, though his Secretary ventured to suggest that, considering the state of the Maharaja's mind, such business transactions might be deferred and that the doctors themselves would not make the slightest objection to that course. Then he shut himself up in his room and gave way to his bursting feelings in solitude. The intensity of his sorrow, however, unmanned him only for the time being, for shortly afterwards he recovered, in great measure, his usual equanimity, self-possession, and philosophic fortitude, as will be evident from the following two letters, the first of which was written the very next day to Babu Nalini Mohan Chakravartti, one of the assistants in his Secretary's office :—

BARIPADA,
10th April, 1906.

MY DEAR NALINI BABU,

I thank you for your very kind letter in the moment of my sorrow. I am reconciled to the situation in which the Almighty Father has placed me. Although the world may look dark and the heart will ache for a time, yet in God's universe, there is nothing evil, and all things work for the glory of God.

Yours sincerely,
S. R. C. B. DEO.

The second letter was written to Babu Nanda Lal Banerjee, a Brahmo gentleman residing at Balasore. It is as follows :—

BARIPADA,
13th April, 1906.

MY DEAR NANDA BABU,

I am sorry I have not been able to reply to your kind message of sympathy. Yes, after every effort had been made to save her life the little angel fled Heavenwards. Of course her departure has left an indelible wound, but who can say that our loss has not been her gain. That must be so, for the dispensations of Providence work for good, although, to our limited vision, they are unmeaning and look dark like the nectar-bearing clouds of summer.

Perhaps she had fulfilled her mission for which she was born and was called away to a higher mansion. She gave up her life in order that her father and other near and dear relations may be carried nearer to their God. From this standpoint the Christian doctrine of atonement is of deep significance. We have to bow to the inevitable with martyr-like resignation and fortitude. I am glad to hear you are improving in health.

Yours sincerely,

S. R. C. B. Deo.

In the two letters quoted above, written during the first outburst of sorrow, when an ordinary man is quite overcome, there is no murmur against fate, not a word of sentimental grief or complaint against the cruel decree of Providence. On the contrary they show the true and steadfast heart of the man and speak volumes for his robust optimism and his firm faith in the wise dispensations of an almighty and benevolent God. Here is no mere preaching or professing religion, but a true and living faith.

This robust optimism finds a still more beautiful expression eight months later in his address, delivered in Calcutta in December, 1906, as President of the Reception Committee of the All-India Theistic Conference, from which we make the following extract, the entire address being reprinted as an Appendix to this book :—

" It is, however, in the moment of sorrow—of that deep sorrow which is the lot of man—when heaven and earth seem an utter blank, an empty void—when the heart is wounded with many wounds—when the mind finds no rest except in the cry of a passionate prayer to God—it is in that critical yet blessed moment that man hears distinctly a voice whispering words of hope and love ; then, too, he receives support and strength to bear all the suffering which the world can inflict ; then, too, he begins to feel that sorrow is a sacrament. He who has realised all this holds in his hands a key to the enigma of life. The world, to such an one, is no longer a fortuitous concourse of atoms, but a divinely designed habitat of living beings ; human beings are no longer the playthings of blind fatalistic forces, but the offspring of God after his own image."

It is worth noting here, as indicating another phase of the high character of the Maharaja, a striking feature of the two letters quoted above which may impress many. Both these letters are written to ordinary individuals—one a subordinate officer in the State and the other a humble gentleman not occupying any high rank or position in life. The Maharaja did not consider it beneath his dignity to acknowledge receipt of their letters and write to them in a friendly manner as man to man—a trait which is very rare in a man of his high position in this country. Evidently he clearly understood and acted according to the noble teaching of Burns :—

> " The rank is but the guinea stamp,
> The man's the gowd [gold] for a' that."

Nothing more surely indicates the true nobility of his character than this sympathetic consideration for the feelings of all men, whether of high or of low estate and his appreciation of their character and motives at their true value, irrespective of rank.

The memory of his daughter was perpetuated by the Maharaja in the Sripad Manjari Memorial Stone erected at the Baripada Leper Asylum, and unveiled on the 18th November, 1907, by Mrs. Bailey during her visit to the State with her husband Mr. W. C. Bailey, Superintendent of the Mission to Lepers in India and the East ; and her name is thus fittingly connected with a noble and philanthropic institution which in its benevolent purpose perpetuates in a manner the promise of her qualities of head and heart. The Asylum was founded in 1896 when a group of thatched huts was made over to Miss J. M. Gilbert for the shelter of the lepers whom she tended. But in this year 1907, the Maharaja erected well-ventilated and useful buildings on a suitable site about two miles from Baripada, where the lepers were comfortably housed and cared for. From its very foundation the institution was under the direct management of the Honorary Secretary, Mrs. Kiddell, who was its life and soul. Her good work is still continued by Miss Allanby, of the Queensland Mission, at Baripada, whose philanthropic works in times of distress caused by flood, famine, or pestilence in Orissa are generally appreciated by a large number of people.

CHAPTER X.

EXTENSION OF HIS POWERS—ARRANGEMENT FOR THE EDUCATION OF HIS CHILDREN—HIS FOREIGN TRAVELS—THE TITLE OF HEREDITARY MAHARAJA CONFERRED ON HIM BY GOVERNMENT.

WHEN the Maharaja assumed the reins of administration in 1892 he had naturally only very limited powers. The powers which could be exercised by a Feudatory Chief had not been accurately prescribed at that time, and the question of their definition was placed before Government for consideration, with the result that the powers of each Chief were defined and limited by the terms of the Sanads granted to them in 1894. The Maharaja's wise, careful, and just exercise of these limited powers, and his sound knowledge of law and procedure, justified and obtained for him their extension by Government, and consequently the full powers of a Session Judge were conferred on him towards the end of the year 1908, much to the gratification not only of himself but of his subjects These full powers were at the same time, with the approval of Government, delegated to the State

Judge, Babu Haridas Bose, B.L., an officer whose ability and integrity merited the assumption of his capability of exercising such extensive jurisdiction. Thereafter all serious criminal cases were tried by the State Judge, the Maharaja, as President of his Judicial Committee, sitting as a first Court of Appeal.

About this time the Maharaja began to make provision for the further education of his children. They had hitherto been taught privately and had received a good grounding in elementary subjects and acquired a sound knowledge of English, not only at Baripada but also in Hazaribagh and Darjeeling, to which places they had been sent at different periods for the benefit of their health. The Maharaja was desirous not only that they should receive as good an education as possible, but also that they should receive a training such as might best fit them for their duties in life and turn them out manly gentlemen fit to take their proper position in the world. After having carefully considered the best means of attaining this end he sent his two boys, along with their cousin, to the Mayo College at Ajmer in the beginning of 1909, in charge of the present writer as tutor and guardian, and of Pandit Dinabandhu Kar as Uriya teacher. He arranged that his two sons should reside with one of the English masters at the College and that, while scrupulously observing all the ceremonies and rites of Hindu religion and caste, they should in all other respects live and be brought up as English boys are, for he was of opinion that only in this way could they acquire that sturdiness of character and polish of manner which he so much desired in them. The wisdom of his choice of schools and of his policy regarding his sons' education has been fully justified by its results, and the boys bid fair to be worthy sons of their most worthy father.

This important matter settled he was free to carry out a project on which he had long set his heart, but which he had been unable to undertake owing in part to his reluctance to leave his children unprovided for at home and in part to the multifarious cares of State. He had always had a keen desire to visit foreign lands, not as a pleasure-seeking globe-trotter, but as an earnest student, to study the men and manners of those civilised nations which occupy the foremost place in the world of thought and action: to study on the spot their laws and institutions, their arts and industries, their improved methods of agriculture, education, sanitation—in a word, the causes and conditions of their material and moral prosperity, which has made such rapid strides in recent years. This he desired not in a spirit of idle curiosity, but in order that he might better fit himself for the government of his own territory and learn how best he might take measures for its improvement and advancement.

With this object in view he prepared a programme for an extensive tour round the world, and on the 8th May, 1910, he set sail for Japan, accompanied by Dr. Debendra Chandra Aich, L.M.S., Chief Medical Officer of the State, and a few attendants and servants. He reached Hongkong on the 25th May and lunched with the Governor on the 27th. He visited Canton on the 28th in order to have a glimpse of China, and on his return from there became the guest of Sir Hormushji Modi, the millionaire stockbroker of Hongkong. On the 3rd June he dined with the Governor of the Island, and on the following day re-embarked for Shanghai, touching at Nagasaki on the 9th, and arriving at Yokohama on the 13th June. Thence he proceeded to Tokyo, where he and his party received an enthusiastic welcome on their arrival, on 15th June, at the Shimbashi Station from the members of the Indo-Japanese Association. His Excellency Sir Claud MacDonald visited the Maharaja and they exchanged cordial greetings. Thereafter he spent an interesting and profitable ten days visiting such of the local institutions and scenes as he could compass in the time at his disposal. On the 16th he inspected the Tokyo Technical School and the Commercial Museum and paid a visit to the West Hongwanji Temple at Tsabiji. Next day he visited the Women's University, the Peers' School, Professor Kono's Jujitsu School, and the University Botanical Gardens. On the afternoon of the 18th he left for Nikko and returned to Tokyo on the 22nd, after having made a tour of, among other things, the Nikko Temples, Kegon Fall, and Lake Chuzenji.

On the 23rd he visited the Imperial Museum and attended a Japanese theatrical performance at Kobukiza. On the morning of the 24th he saw the Civil and Military Museum.

The next few days were occupied with public functions, at which the Maharaja was the honoured guest, and of which we extract the following account from the "Japan" newspaper, dated 28th June, 1910:—

"His Highness the Maharaja of Mayurbhanj was entertained at a tea party in Count Okuma's garden on Friday, the 24th instant. On that occasion the Indo-Japanese Association presented him with the following address which was read by the Vice-President, Baron Kanda:—

"'His Highness Maharaja Sri Ram Chandra Bhanj Deo, Mayurbhanj:

May it please your Highness—

We, the President and Members of the Indo-Japanese Association, deem it a high honour to welcome your Highness to this Land of the Rising Sun. The genuine interest your Highness takes in the welfare of your subjects is keenly appreciated by us, and your sympathetic, progressive, and enlightened rule has won our deep respect and approbation.

"This is the first visit with which we have been honoured by the ruler of a State in Orissa, and we earnestly hope that it may prove of interest to your Highness and of advantage to your subjects. We are confident that such visits from Ruling Chiefs, which we expect to be more frequent every year, cannot fail to render more cordial and intimate the friendly relations between the people of India and Japan.

"Wishing your Highness a very pleasant sojourn in this country and long life and happiness in your native land, we have the honour to be, etc.

Shigenobu Okuma, President, and Members of
the Indo-Japanese Association.

Tokyo, June 24th, 1910.'

" A beautiful silver casket containing the address was then presented to the Maharaja, who in reply stated that India had much to learn from Japan and that he would advise his brother Chiefs in Orissa to pay visits to this Land of the Rising Sun. He remarked that he was very much pleased with his visit to this beautiful country and he had been the recipient of so many acts of kindness during his stay here that he felt quite at home. The Maharaja concluded by thanking the Association for the address presented to him.

"On Saturday the 25th, the Indo-Japanese Association gave a Japanese dinner in honour of the

Maharaja Sri Ram Chandra and Members, Indo-Japanese Association, Tokio

Front row, right to left of picture.—Mr. Kaka, Mr. Matsno, *Manager, Yokohama Specie Bank*, Baron Kanda, Dr. Aich, Count Okuma, MAHARAJA OF MAYURBHANJ, Baron Shibusawa, Mr. Besamia, Vicount Fuknoka, *Professor, Peers' College*, Mr. Desai.

Back row, from right to left of picture.—Mr. Sujoshi, Mr. Sakurai, *Editor*, "*Sinkiron*", Professor Shiozawa, *Wasida University*, Mr. Setna, Mr. Besamia, Mr. Heroi, *Secretary, I. J. Assoc.*, Mr. Sœjiwa, Mr. Edalji, *Secretary, I. J. Assoc.*, Dr. Tokakasu, *Professor, Tokio Imperial University*, Mr. Sugamura, *Editor*, "*Asaki*", Mr. Tanie, *Assistant Secretary, I. J. Assoc.*, Mr. Yamada, *Editor*, "*Munich.*"

Maharaja at the Tokiwa Kwadan, Uyeno Park. At the end of the dinner, Count Okuma, President of the Association, called for three banzais for His Highness which were cordially given. His Highness thanked the President and Members of the Association for the kindness shown to him. He further said that he admired this country and its people so much that, according to the Buddhistic belief in re-birth, he would like to be born a Japanese at the next birth. His Highness noticed that one of the main objects of the Association was to promote friendly relations between Japan and India and he exhorted the Indian merchants present and others to do all in their power to render these friendly relations still more cordial and intimate.

" On Sunday the 26th, Baron Shibusawa entertained the Maharaja at luncheon and with Japanese music at his Asukayama villa. His Highness remarked that Japanese music had much in common with Indian music. The Baron then showed the Maharaja over his garden, which, being exquisitely laid out, was much admired.

" On Monday morning the 27th, His Highness was received in audience by His Majesty the Emperor. On the same afternoon, accompanied by Dr. Aich, he left for Kyoto. After visiting Kyoto, Nara, Osaka, and Nagoya, His Highness will arrive at Yokohama on the 4th July."

So ends the account given in the "Japan" of these pleasant functions. Thereafter the Maharaja completed his tour of the country as outlined above, finding much of interest and profit and not a little pleasure therein, and then sailed for America, in the steamer "Mauretania," Dr. Aich at this point leaving him and proceeding home to Baripada. The Maharaja arrived in London on the 22nd August, where he joined the Maharani, who had sailed direct to England with her sister the Maharani of Cooch Behar at about the same time as her husband left for Japan. A brief account of the journey from Japan to America and thence to England has been given by himself in his letter to Dr. Aich, dated London, 31st August, 1910, for permission to use which and other material connected with the Maharaja's tour our thanks are due to the doctor :—

"After we parted in Japan my trip has been uneventful. The passage across the Pacific has been very calm and quiet and there is nothing very much to record except that in Mid-Pacific it became very cold on account of the northerly course we took. In Vancouver I was very hospitably received by Dr. Monroe, the Port Medical Officer. I broke journey at Laggan and Banff in the Rockies, at Winnipeg, and then *viâ* the great lakes to Toronto. I then went across to the Niagara Falls and then by river route on the St. Lawrence to Montreal and Quebec. I had to rush through America and the long railway and steamer journeys were somewhat tiresome. The people, however, were very kind and hospitable everywhere. I had to prolong my stay in New York for about nine days. Here I was the guest of Mr. and Mrs. Perin for four days, who introduced me to several well-known people. I had an opportunity of seeing the Bethlehem Steel Works and the Schenectady Electric Works. From New York I came by the "Lusitania," the sistership of the "Mauretania." The passage across the Atlantic was even calmer than across the Pacific and was uneventful. I arrived in London on the 22nd instant. The climate of England is very good, much like that of Darjeeling in September. There is a good deal of rain and the sky is almost always overclouded. . . . .

"I am taking rest in this quiet place which is about twelve miles off from London. I went to the India Office on the 24th and saw Mr. Hirtzel, the Political Secretary. I am going there again to-morrow and will meet the officials. I expect to see Lord Morley and Their Majesties before leaving London. . . . .

"We are all quite well. The servants are quite at home. Rice, dâl, 'masalas,' and all things found in India are found here. Even Ganges water can be found if search is made for it. Have met Mr. K. G. Gupta and the Gaekwar."

In another letter to Dr. Aich, dated Norbiton Hall, London Road, Kingston, 10th October, 1910, he writes that he was just returned from a nursing home in London where he had undergone a slight but somewhat painful operation and had been confined to bed for about a fortnight. In the same letter he writes: "I am afraid I shall have hardly any time to go to the Continent. I propose paying my respects to Their Majesties during this month, and also see other prominent men and then see Parliament when it opens. I leave England on the 4th December and will arrive in Bombay about the end of the month."

In a letter to the present writer, dated 9th September, the Maharaja writes from London:—

"I have had a most interesting tour through China, Japan, and America, and have now settled down here for a little rest and quiet. I have improved greatly in health and spirits and hope to go back rejuvenated. The English climate is most bracing and delightful. In fact the climate of all the places I have visited is good and brings forcibly home to my mind the truth that climate is a great national asset and the Indian climate compares most unfavourably with those of all prosperous countries. The Japanese and Americans are charming people bubbling over with the milk of human feelings. To strangers they are particularly hospitable and courteous and nowhere did I receive anything but kindness. These are wonderful people and have a great future before them."

During his tour abroad the management of the State was undertaken by Mr. L. E. B. Cobden Ramsay, I.C.S., Political Agent of the Orissa Feudatory States, who became President of the State Council, and the confidence of the Maharaja in him is expressed in the following extract from a letter to Dr. Aich written from London :—

" I am glad to learn that the Political Agent is taking so much interest in the affairs of the State. I am sure, under his supervision, things will go on very well and there will be very little room for intrigue."

The fact that he had been enabled to make such fortunate provision for the care of the State during his absence had been one of the chief factors in setting him free to make the world-tour which he was thereby able to undertake with an easy mind knowing that things could not go wrong during his absence.

Without this kind assistance his dutiful conscience would scarcely have permitted him to absent himself so long.

During his absence the hereditary title of Maharaja was conferred on him by Government in recognition of the high qualities of his personal character and ability and of his efficient and successful administration of the State, and the Sanad investing him with this unsolicited but highly valued honour was presented to him on his return to India by Sir Edward Baker, Lieutenant-Governor of Bengal, who expressed in most cordial terms the appreciation of Government of his able and public-spirited management of his State, and his charity and liberality not only towards local objects but to all other institutions such as appealed to his generosity. After the investiture he returned to Baripada, in the beginning of 1911, to the great joy of his people, who gave him a most enthusiastic welcome and presented him with an address which we reproduce as showing the regard in which he was generally held :—

" May it please your Highness—

" We, the Members of the Raj family, the people and servants of the State, all united and animated with most sincere feelings of joy and happiness, respectfully beg leave to approach your Highness to accord a most loyal and heartfelt welcome on this very happy occasion of your safe return to your territory after a long sojourn in foreign lands.

" Since your assumption of the reins of administration of the State, your Highness worked incessantly and strenuously for the advancement of the people committed to your charge, without taking any rest and without minding the strain and worry attending it and their injurious effect upon your health.

"We also offer our humble thanks to the All-Merciful Providence, whose blessings had been on you in your travels, far and wide, on sea and lands, and Who has brought you home safe with perfectly renewed health, amongst your loving and expectant subjects.

"We take this opportunity of publicly expressing deep gratitude to the just, generous, and discerning British Government for conferring the hereditary distinction of Maharaja on you.

"We need hardly recount here the various good measures initiated by your Highness to promote the welfare of your subjects and the many inestimable boons conferred upon them, who feel happy and contented under your just and beneficent administration and are lovingly and devotedly attached to your person. Your Highness's single-minded devotion to duty, noble self-sacrificing spirit, inimitable amiableness, saintly purity of heart and life, high attainments in different branches of useful knowledge, and great solicitude for the good of humanity have justly earned for you the high and honourable distinction of being an ideal ruler of a Native State.

"Your travels in foreign countries, which have enabled you to recruit your health, have at the same time greatly widened your experience of men and things. They have brought you in personal contact with great men of some of the most advanced countries in the world and enabled you to acquire a first-hand knowledge of the working of a good many useful institutions in these countries. The vast experience gained by your Highness during your foreign travels will be greatly helpful to you in initiating and carrying out various measures for improving the condition of your subjects, whose welfare you have always at heart.

"May God grant you a long, happy, useful, and prosperous life and shower upon you His choicest blessings, is the earnest prayer of

Your Highness's

Most Loyal and Loving Subjects."

CHAPTER XI.

THE DELHI DURBAR—HIS ACTIVE INTEREST IN THE CALCUTTA PAGEANT—HIS DEATH BY ACCIDENT.

BY a most unfortunate stroke of fate the State was deprived of that opportunity for improved development and progress, to undertake which the Maharaja had qualified himself by his visit to foreign lands and study of their industries and institutions. Shortly after his return home, the announcement of Their Imperial Majesties' intended visit to India caused a great sensation and gave rise to an outburst of loyalty and rejoicing unprecedented in the annals of this country; for the occasion was an unique one and hence the demonstration of joy, too, was unparalleled. The Maharaja threw himself heart and soul into the task of preparing his share in the entertainment of Their Majesties, and during this period, though he continued to supervise the work of the State with his accustomed ability and zeal, he was unable to take up the active development of many of the new schemes on which he had set his heart; and before he had a full opportunity to do so death set a seal on his earthly endeavours.

The programme of the Calcutta pageant on the occasion of the gracious visit of their Imperial Majesties to that city, included a War Dance by the Uriya paiks, the organization and management of which was entrusted to the Maharaja of Mayurbhanj as he had an expert knowledge of the Uriya national dances, and it was his people chiefly who were to take part in the war dance. The labour entailed in this was very great, as not only had the appropriate costumes and arms to be studied and arranged for, but the performers, many of whom were new recruits, had to be trained in their parts almost from the beginning. For months the Maharaja with indefatigable energy trained the men and personally attended the rehearsals which took place twice daily. It was a sight to see how he with his brother, the Rautrai Saheb, and his cousins laboured with the paiks, giving them verbal and practical instructions in that difficult and intricate act which requires strenuous exercise of every limb and puts a great strain on the muscles. The result justified the great trouble and minute attention to detail given to the matter by the Chief: Maharaja Sir Pradyot Kumar Tagore and Mr. Frank R. Lascelles, master of the pageant, attended the final rehearsal at Baripada and were highly pleased with the performance. Mr. Lascelles who had great experience of all such ceremonies remarked that it was the most interesting and lively item in the whole

Minor Maharaja Purno Chandra Bhanj Deo.

programme of the pageant. Later on Their Imperial Majesties themselves expressed their satisfaction at the warlike performance of the paiks, and the King Emperor made special reference to this in his letter of the 24th February, 1912, to the Viceroy of India in which he graciously expressed his personal regret at the Maharaja's death, saying: "The Queen and I are grieved to hear of the death by an accident of the Maharaja of Mayurbhanj. Please convey to the Maharani our sincere condolences with her in her sorrow. We remember, of course, the important part taken by the Maharaja in connection with the pageant on the maidan and our pleasure in seeing him on that occasion."

The Maharaja, with the Maharani and the Maharaj Kumars, attended the Delhi Durbar which took place on the 12th December, 1911, and had the honour of making his obeisance to the King-Emperor. Thereafter he came back to Calcutta to make the final arrangements for the pageant, which was a brilliant success. His eldest son and heir, Purno Chandra, was one of Her Majesty's pages on that historic occasion. No one could dream for a moment amid these unprecedented gatherings of illustrious personages and during these dazzling scenes of superb magnificence in which he had taken so prominent a part, that his brilliant career with its lofty aspirations would be so tragically terminated so soon after their close.

He returned to Baripada full of the idea of setting on foot those new schemes of development which he had formulated in the past two years. One of the chief of these was to extend the Mayurbhanj State Railway into the forests in the heart of the State in order to be able to exploit more fully and economically the vast quantities of timber to be found there. With this object in view he invited some officials of the Bengal-Nagpur Railway to inspect the route. On the 30th January, these gentlemen with some relations of the Maharaja went out on a shooting excursion, but bagged no game; so next day the Maharaja himself went with them to ensure that they should get good sport. The beat took place in a jungle near Baripada about three miles from Krishnachandrapur Station. One bear was killed and one was believed to have been wounded but to have escaped. The beat had not yet finished when, as fate would have it, the Maharaja, though thoroughly acquainted with the rules of sport, descended from his machan, in spite of the earnest entreaties of his faithful attendant, Radhu Mahapatra, not to do so till the beaters should have come up. The Maharaja, however, paid no attention to the warning and when he got down his attendant followed him. He was wearing a black suit at the time and the occupant of the next machan, mistaking his figure in the dim light for that of the wounded bear, fired.

The bullet hit Radhu on the knee and, before the Maharaja could ascertain the cause of his agonising cry, another bullet hit a tree close by himself and splinters entered both his hands and chest. For a moment he was dazed by the shock, but just then the other members of the party, attracted by Radhu's cry, hurried up and anxiously attended to him, sending a messenger post-haste for the doctor. But such was the Maharaja's nobility of soul that, when he saw that all people had naturally flocked round him and were trying to render him what assistance they could under the circumstances, he repeatedly said to them, " Why do you all come to me? Why don't you go and look after poor Radhu?" showing anxious solicitude for the sufferings of another even when he himself was enduring acute pain.

The present writer who was in Baripada at the time will never forget the scene which followed. We were sitting with Dr. Aich in the afternoon when a motor-car conveying Lal Saheb Girish Chandra Bhanj Deo came tearing up and halted at the door. In feverish excitement he broke the news to us and hurried the doctor in his motor to the scene of the accident. The news of the occurrence spread like wildfire and the consternation which it caused was painful. Men of all classes and communities began to run towards the station in wildest excitement and gravest anxiety; women and children ran to each other's houses or to the Diwan's house for reassuring news. After about an hour's terrible suspense the Diwan motored back through the town proclaiming aloud the good news that the Maharaja was doing well and was coming in a carriage to Belgaria Palace. This allayed the panic and anxiety to some extent, but none had any peace that night. The Civil Surgeon of Balasore was brought up by a special train that evening, and next morning the people of Mayurbhanj learned with a sigh of relief that the Maharaja's wounds were not at all serious. His attendant, who had been conveyed to Baripada Hospital, succumbed in the morning, but the Maharaja progressed favourably and nobody suspected that the end was so near.

But in an unfortunate hour he came down to Calcutta, not so much for treatment as to keep some engagements, one of which was to invite a certain high official to Mayurbhanj in connection with a projected scheme of making Meghasani Hill, the highest peak in the State, a sanatorium for Orissa and the summer residence of His Honour the Lieutenant-Governor of the newly created province of Bihar and Orissa. An X-ray examination made in Calcutta revealed that splinters of the bullet were lying embedded both in his hands and in his chest. An operation was performed under chloroform and the splinters were extracted, but symptoms of blood-poisoning set in; and in spite of all efforts to save him, the Maharaja died of these after-effects of the wound on the morning of the 22nd February, 1912.

His death was as heroic as tragic. He retained his consciousness almost to the end, and with Stoic endurance and calm resignation awaited the final dissolution, defying excruciating physical pain without a groan or a murmur. He shed no tears and uttered no complaint against fate, but with a smiling countenance passed away like a saint and a hero. A few minutes only before his death, when the Diwan entered the room, the dying man greeted him with a smile, having by that time lost the power of speech. Those who saw him after death could hardly believe that he was no more: the same characteristic sweet smile was still upon his lips, and he lay as if asleep, and in his sleep had seen a beautiful vision which thrilled his soul with peace and happiness. While he lived he taught by personal example how to conquer earthly vanities and desires—when he died he taught how to conquer death itself, the grim and awful king of terrors. His philosophical and religious studies were not in vain; the lofty teachings of the Vedanta philosophy supported him in stress and strain in his death as well as in life.

The following poem composed by the present writer immediately after the death of the Maharaja was approved and very favourably spoken of by Mr. Cobden Ramsay, I.C.S., the Political Agent of the Orissa Feudatory States, and may, therefore, not inappropriately close this sad chapter :—

It's all a dream ! Art thou really no more
O' dearly loved Chief, with wisdom deep,
So great yet gracious, good, all virtues' store,
Art thou really hushed in eternal sleep ?

See our bleeding hearts, where thou art enshrined,
Enthroned, as a Saint and Sage, so pure, profound,
So simple, yet with such a lofty mind
And tender heart—a glorious, rare compound.

O' prince of men, for what offence so dire
Hast thou left us so early ? Oh, the blow
Has stunned us quite ! Come back, beloved sire
To wipe a nation's tears which ceaseless flow.

Alas, we wretched souls are left behind,
But heartless Fate thy useful life couldn't spare.
God's will we dare not scan nor call unkind,
But oh ! this sudden shock what man can bear ?

Soul never dies we know, but what solace
That thought, to crushed and broken hearts, can give ?
We long to see that noble smiling face,
We want that angel in our midst to live.

Angels of light a lot in Heaven there are,
But mother earth has few such godlike sons ;
Who can annihilate their "self" so far
As did our Chief who lived for other ones ;

Who always said that man is born to work,
And who himself did practise what he preached ;
From work however hard who ne'er would shirk
But record bright, with brilliant deeds enriched.

Still blows the breeze, still stand the hoary hills,
Still flowers bloom, and birds as usual sing,

The world still goes, still onward flow the rills,
    All things are same ! we miss one heavenly being.

The guide is gone, the lamp no longer burns,
    The path before us dark and dreary lies ;
The heart is sick and faint and fondly turns
    To thy mem'ry sweet with hopeless heavy sighs.

In holier halo shine in regions bright
    And pour down dazzling chast'ning ray divine,
In drooping hearts infuse effulgent light,
    Thy glory here below shall ever shine.

CHAPTER XII.

Maharaja Sri Ram Chandra as an Administrator—His Policy and His Ideals.

In the third chapter we have briefly outlined the results of the rule of Maharaja Krishna Chandra Bhanj Deo and showed how he took the first steps to introduce the beginnings of order and method in the administration of the State where previously no system can be said to have existed. Further progress was made in the same direction by Mr. Wylly during the ten years' period of Government management which followed the death of that Chief, and a solid foundation was laid on which the elaborate edifice of modern statecraft could be raised. It was left for Maharaja Sri Ram Chandra to raise that structure, and it is to his everlasting credit that he fully realized his responsibilities and opportunities, taking up without faltering the burden of the task laid upon him, and leaving no stone unturned, no chance neglected, whereby he might improve his heritage in every respect and thereby add to the well-being and prosperity of every kind and class of its inhabitants. His whole life was single-mindedly directed towards that end and while, being human, he made some mistakes and had to record some failures (due in part to his being in some respects far ahead of his times), the net result of his labours was to raise the status of Mayurbhanj from a mere "Jungle Mahal" of Orissa to be the leading State in that province and one of the best governed Native States in India.

He wasted no time in settling to his duties. After his two years' period of probation he took up immediately the problem of organizing the machinery of government in the form which he considered best for the State and most calculated to ensure efficient administration and the dispensation of pure and even-handed justice. Nothing shows so clearly the high quality of his ideals and his determination to give the State the best that was in him as the deliberate limitation of his own powers by the quasi-constitutional policy which he adopted from the beginning of his rule. He realised at once that he was no more infallible than other men and that he could best guard against mistakes and accomplish more and better work by taking counsel with such of his officers and others as were best qualified by knowledge and experience to aid him with their advice. With this object he established in 1892-93 the Mayurbhanj State Council. This consisted of the Maharaja as President, four official members, namely, the Diwan, the State Judge, the

State Engineer, and the Superintendent of Police, and two non-official members, who were at that time Chotarai Brindaban Chandra Bhanj Deo and Bebarta Ram Hari Jit Babu, all nominated by the Chief. Its constitution varied from time to time as circumstances necessitated, but throughout the Maharaja's time it was responsible for the drawing up of all the legislative acts promulgated in the State and of orders and rules for the guidance of the various departments, while it also dealt with matters concerning the finances of the State and considered and settled the provisions of the annual budget; and while the Maharaja remained the ruling and directing spirit of its deliberations, there is no doubt that he obtained very great assistance in all matters connected with State policy from the members of which the council was composed from time to time.

One of the first measures of the newly created council was to introduce into the State the Criminal and Civil Codes of British India, which had heretofore been followed to some extent in spirit but by no means in letter. Thereafter every year there were added other rules and regulations making provision for new circumstances which arose with the growth of the State in prosperity and of its management in complexity. Such were the tenancy laws, laws relating to survey and settlement of land revenue, limitation acts, regulations introducing the use of court fees and regulating the sale of stamps, providing for the registration of documents, the administration of Hindu religious endowments, the control of emigration, the exclusion of undesirables, the organization of rural police, the introduction and possession of arms and explosives, and many others too numerous to mention. The admiration with which the Maharaja regarded the laws of British India, resulting from his close study of history and of law and his recognition of the principles of justice and equity on which they are founded and which is their chief characteristic, led him to adopt in their entirety such of these laws as were most suited to the needs of his people and his times and to modify others in a manner best adapted to local conditions; and the laws so promulgated were not unchangeable like those of the ancient Medes and Persians, but were amended, improved, and extended from time to time as experience of local requirements gradually matured.

Simultaneously with the creation of a body of laws he organized practically from the beginning the departmental machinery necessary to administer it. From small beginnings this machinery was elaborated as need arose, till it assumed the proportions and practically the form and quality of the organization of a British district. The judicial and executive departments were separated as far as was compatible with the proper distribution of the work to be done, and separate departments were inaugurated for the disposal of civil and criminal work, management of the revenue and cases arising under that head, survey and settlement, treasury and police, etc. While the separation of the judicial and executive functions was more or less completely effected in the Sadar subdivision, it was not so in the two outlying subdivisions,—a third was created towards the close of his rule,—where the subdivisional officer continued to unite in his own hands, within due limits, all the powers of a civil and criminal court as well as those of an executive officer. Later, when he attained full power, the Maharaja carried out on the judicial side the same principle of limitation of his authority as he had previously effected on the legislative side, and united with himself the Diwan to form a Judicial Committee, which sat as a First Court of Appeal from judgments of the State Judge, and also exercised powers of revision over the decision of all courts. By this separation of judicial and executive functions the Maharaja rendered his own executive orders liable to be called in question and perhaps upset in the civil courts, but he deliberately introduced this innovation in order that a further safeguard might be provided against the possibility of his making mistakes, and he would on occasion admit with perfect equanimity his own error when appeals in such cases came before the Judicial Committee. The principle was admirable, and his recognition and admission of it remarkable in a man in his position; but there is no doubt that in this respect he was too far ahead of his time. His people were not sufficiently advanced properly to appreciate and to use this privilege granted to them, of contesting the validity of their Chief's own orders.

At the time of his death the organization of the machinery of administration was briefly as follows:—There were four subdivisions—Sadar, Bahmanghatti, Panchpir, and Kaptipada. The outlying subdivisions were each in charge of an officer who exercised the magisterial powers of a subdivisional officer as defined in the Criminal Procedure Code, and also limited powers as a munsiff, and was the chief executive authority within his jurisdiction. At Sadar, the place of the subdivisional officer was taken by the State collector, who had, however, no civil powers. The Maharaja retained in his own hand the chief executive authority and kept direct control over the police, public works, forests, education, and medical departments, but delegated to the Diwan full powers as a revenue officer and made him head of the Revenue Department, including settlement, agriculture, and zemindari matters. The Diwan exercised all the powers of a collector. Under him were the State collector, a staff of deputy collectors, and the sub-divisional officers in their capacity of deputy collectors. The State judge was the head of the judicial side of the administration and controlled the sub-judge and all the magistrates and the sub-divisional officers in their capacities of deputy magistrates and munsiffs. In civil cases the State judge exercised the powers of a district judge in British India, and in 1908 was vested, with the approval of Government, with the full powers of a sessions judge. Appeals against his decision lay to the Judicial Committee.

For the better enforcing of the criminal law, the Police Department was reorganized on modern lines from its foundations and placed under the charge of Mr. Kiddell. There was at that time only the nucleus of a regular police staff, most of the work being done by local sardars, who had no training and very little aptitude for the work. The village chaukidars, where they existed, were supported entirely by voluntary contributions from the villagers and were under no sort of discipline and control. This was all done away with; the sardars, except in one special instance, were deprived of their police powers and a regular system of thanas and outposts gradually established and staffed by properly qualified officers and men. The chaukidars were also gradually brought under control, and later a chaukidari tax was assessed for their regular payment in place of the primitive method of payment by voluntary contributions. An effort was also made to introduce the union system into the Sadar subdivision, but this was not very successful at first, owing to the difficulty of finding suitable panchayats. By 1910-11 there were 13 thanas, and 10 outposts in the State and the total strength of the police force, excluding village chaukidars was 65 officers and 272 men.

To carry on the work of these various administrative departments, the Maharaja reorganized his staff, doing his best to obtain men of education and ability. Previously the work of the State had been done by officers who had more or less a sort of hereditary title to their posts and who were poorly paid, sometimes getting, as an additional reward for good work, land or villages assigned to them revenue-free on occasions of special rejoicing. This primitive system of recruitment and reward was done away with and a regularly graded service brought into being with good pay and prospects for good work; and to make the State service still more attractive, a pension system was inaugurated in 1894-95, whereby all officers above a certain grade had to contribute a very small proportion of their monthly salary to the pension fund, thereby ensuring themselves on their retirement a substantial pension, the greater proportion of which was paid by the State. A competent and trustworthy staff, both of officers and subordinates, was thus gradually secured, capable of appreciating and working hard to attain the aims of their Chief, and secure in the knowledge that good work was certain of its due reward.

CHAPTER XIII.

THE MAHARAJA AS AN ADMINISTRATOR (*continued*)—IMPROVEMENT OF THE CONDITIONS OF HIS PEOPLE.

SIMULTANEOUSLY with his inauguration of reforms of the form and machinery of administration, the Maharaja made a beginning of his policy of government for the people by granting in 1892 to all his tenants a right of occupancy in their holdings. Previously land had been held subject to the will of the Chief and no man had a right to sell, mortgage, or bequeath his holding; he was merely a tenant-at-will and could not be secure even that he would be allowed to cultivate from year to year, though, on the whole, instances of unjust eviction were naturally rare. The right of occupancy now granted, altered all this. It gave the tenant a security which he had never known before, raising his status and credit and enabling him to exploit his land to the best of his ability, putting him in a position of certainty that he and his children would continue to reap their crops from year to year so long as they continued to pay the rent due to the State. This most important and far-reaching reform was the first of many measures intended to improve the prospects of the people and ensure not only their material but their moral happiness and prosperity. Under the name of the Mayurbhanj Tenancy Regulation the system was improved and extended from time to time as circumstances suggested, so as to secure to raiyats of all classes and races the full enjoyment of their rights and liberties and of the proceeds of their labour. One of its important provisions was the exemption of the house and homestead land of a raiyat from attachment and sale in execution of a decree, so that, even if his land were sold up for debt or arrears of rent, his house still remained to him as a shelter to enable him to make a fresh start in life.

That the rights and liberties so provided for might be the better assured, an elaborate system of land survey and settlement was evolved, to take the place of the primitive methods of measurement and assessment previously in vogue. At first this was done on the Uriya system, the fields being measured by a 'padika,' or rod, and the area and class recorded in a khasra; but not many years later this gave place to the more elaborate and far more accurate system of cadastral survey used in British India. The complete survey of the State was undertaken bit by bit and good maps and correct records prepared for every village. The old and somewhat rough system of assessment of rents was discarded in favour of an accurate calculation based on the quality of the fields and the nature of the crops they were capable of producing. The rents assessed were low and were fixed for a period of 10, 15, or 20 years, according to the varying circumstances of the different parganas, and in subsequent settlements after the expiry of the previous fixed period, the enhancement of rate of rent taken was very small and was based strictly on the amount of rise in the price of food crops and the result of improvements effected by the State. Land was in no case arbitrarily or oppressively assessed. Further, all abwabs, or extra exactions in addition to rent, were abolished, so that the raiyat knew for certain that, when he had paid the rent recorded against his name, the State demand for the year was fully satisfied. The combined result of these measures—the security of tenure provided, the accurate record of rights, the low, regular and fairly assessed rent, in addition to the steps taken to increase the facilities for improvement of land by means of irrigation and leasing out of suitable jungle land—was that cultivation not only extended by leaps and bounds, but improved greatly in quality and intensity, thereby supporting a much greater population and leading to a great rise in the land revenue, which increased almost fourfold during the twenty years of the Maharaja's personal rule.

As a corollary to the improvement of the raiyats' credit, certain safeguards were adopted to ensure that it should not be too greatly abused to their own destruction by the more ignorant and improvident classes. One of these was the enforcement of the ancient Hindu law of Dandapat, whereby a creditor could not realize from a debtor interest to an amount greater than the principal of the original loan. Granaries, locally called hamars, were established at various parts of the State and stocked with paddy, which was lent to the raiyats when required, the borrower repaying in kind at a low rate of interest at the end of the agricultural year; provision was made in the budget every year of considerable amounts as agricultural and land improvement loans to such raiyats as needed them for the purchase of seed and cattle or for the extension or improvement of their holdings, these loans being repayable at a low rate of interest in annual instalments of amounts calculated to suit the circumstances of each borrower. Towards the end of his rule the Maharaja, further to free the tenant from the necessity of having recourse to rapacious moneylenders, tried to introduce a system of co-operative credit societies, but, though one or two of these worked fairly well, the majority were failures, owing to want of proper managers and the opposition of the professional mahajans. He, however, continued to help and encourage them so far as possible, but it is not likely that the system will be developed and extended, as it ought to be, for a number of years to come, until the people generally are educated up to appreciate its great advantages.

Not content with extending the facilities for agriculture on existing lines, the Maharaja further turned his attention to the introduction of new crops and the education of the raiyat in their cultivation. His first venture in this direction was also connected with his endeavour to improve the silk manufacturing industry of the State. With this object he tried to introduce the cultivation of the mulberry tree and the scientific rearing of silk-worms and engaged an expert to organise the work, but for one reason or another this experiment failed. The land taken up for the first mulberry plantation was converted into an agricultural experimental farm, where different methods of treating existing crops and the cultivation of diverse new crops were demonstrated to the leading raiyats and seed distributed among them. This resulted in the introduction of several new crops such as groundnuts, cassava, and various kinds of vegetables into the State. He further tried experiments with cotton and leased a large area to a Calcutta firm for its cultivation on scientific lines. The soil and climate, however, proved unsuitable for the species of cotton tried and the area was subsequently leased to Sir Daniel Hamilton, who devoted part of it to the raising of sisal fibre and to experiments in the growing of rubber.

The Maharaja also devoted some part of his consideration to the non-agricultural population of the State, by endeavouring to better the conditions and improve the output of the few local manufacturing industries which exist. Apart from the usual carpenters, blacksmiths, and weavers, who turn out ordinary utensils and clothes for local use, the most important industry which employs the greatest number of artisans, and the products of which command the widest sale outside the boundaries of the State is the weaving of tassar silk cloth. The attempt to introduce a better quality of raw material by the rearing of the mulberry silkworm proved a failure, as stated above, and the only course left was to improve as far as possible the methods of manufacture of the kind of silk already woven, and, by the provision of better dyes and introduction of new patterns, turn out a better and more varied article which would command a greater market and a higher price. With the assistance of Babu Kamakhya Prasad Bose, Subdivisional Officer of Bahmanghatti, who had an expert knowledge of weaving, and by the advancing of loans to the weavers and grants for the purchase of raw material, a decided advance was made in this direction, and the cloth exhibited at the Calcutta Industrial Exhibition in 1906 and the Jajpur

Agricultural Exhibition in 1910 was much admired and secured a number of prizes. He also encouraged as far as possible the cultivation of lac, and to that end aided the establishment of two lac factories in the Bahmanghatti subdivision, one of which still continues. Again, with the idea of improving the quality and methods of outturn of articles for local use and the training of a body of artisans who would provide for the industrial needs of the State he started a technical school at Baripada, to teach carpentry to begin with, intending that it should embrace blacksmithy, tinsmithy, and other trades, as it developed. Unfortunately, owing to a mistaken policy of giving fixed stipends to the scholars, to bad management, and to apathy of the people in the matter, the school was not a success and was closed down for the time. It was the Maharaja's intention to re-establish it on better and more modern lines, and to this end he studied the organization and management of technical schools in Japan and elsewhere, but was cut off before he could carry his purpose into effect.

He fully recognized the fact that his reforms and improvements could not have their full effect, and that the people would not be able to take advantage of and benefit by them as they ought, until they were educated up to a better standard both of intelligence and of mode of life. For this reason the educational policy of the State was always one of his most anxious cares. The Middle English School at Baripada was raised to the status of a High English School in 1892, and in his resolution on the annual report for the school in 1892-93, he thus states his policy :—" At present no fees are taken, the institution being entirely maintained at the expense of the State. Books, too, are often given to the poor students free of charge. This state of affairs shows that the appreciation for high education has not advanced proportionately with the other industrial advances of the population. Our policy has been, and will be for a long time to come, to force the people to appreciate education." His development of the education system, however, was wisely very gradual. It was not till 1904 that, following the advice of Sir Andrew Fraser, he imposed fees on the scholars attending the Baripada School. He slowly increased the number of schools of various classes throughout the State from 44, which was the total number in the time of his father, to 431 in 1910-11, providing suitable buildings and, most important of all, securing qualified teachers as far as available. The average annual number of scholars attending school increased in the same period from 2,376 to 9,594, and the annual expenditure on education from Rs. 7,899 in 1882 to Rs. 54,958 in 1910. It was his expressed intention, after the system had been fully extended and a sufficient number of properly equipped schools and duly qualified teachers had been provided, to make the acquirement of some standard of education compulsory for all classes and to impose an education cess to meet the great cost of the measure; but the time for introducing it had not yet ripened, when he died.

His measures for the care of the physical health of his people were as thorough and elaborate as those for the care of their mental wellbeing. The following extract from Mr. Wylly's annual report for the year 1882-83 shows the primitive condition of the Medical Department at that time :—"A dispensary existed, but the building was in a dilapidated condition and is now being remodelled. The sanitation of the town of Baripada is very bad; special measures will have to be adopted and taxes imposed before any improvement can be made and the place kept clean and healthy. For the dispensary there is only one hospital assistant, on Rs. 40, and a compounder, on Rs. 10. From what I have experienced I think there should be a good assistant-surgeon appointed. The place is unhealthy; epidemics may break out at any moment." Thereafter Mr. Wylly secured the services of Dr. Purna Chandra Gupta, who remained at the head of the Medical Department till 1903 and put the sanitation of the town and its medical resources on a sound footing; but, handicapped by lack of funds, he was unable to extend medical services to

8

the mofussil; during Maharaja Sri Ram Chandra's time, however, this was developed, till in 1910 there were eight well-equipped dispensaries in the State, including that in the Nayabasan Zamindari, each in charge of a competent medical officer and provided with an excellent stock of medicines and appliances to provide relief to the thousands who attended them in the course of the year. The sanitation report for that year says:—"Public health was good during the year under report. There were only 48 cases of cholera within the jurisdiction of Baisinga, Muruda, and Barsahi thanas. The total expenditure for all dispensaries of the State for the year under report was Rs. 17,032." Just before his death, the Chief undertook the remodelling of the Baripada Hospital and its extension to commemorate the reign of the late King Edward, and the King Edward VII. Charitable Dispensary and Hospital is now a model of what such institutions should be.

Measures were also introduced for the prevention of cholera and smallpox, vaccination against the latter disease being made to all intents and purposes compulsory, with the result that these dread scourges appear only sporadically from time to time and are never allowed to assume epidemic form.

The conservancy department of Baripada, which was formerly responsible for the cleanliness and health of the town, was merged into the Baripada

Municipality, which was established in the year 1905. A regular constitution was drawn up by the Maharaja on the lines of the Municipal Act in force in British India, and a chairman and 15 commissioners, of whom 6 were official and 9 non-official, were appointed to form a Municipal Committee with full powers to look after the sanitation of the town, in addition to the making and repairing of roads, street cleaning, lighting, etc., and to assess taxes to provide the necessary funds for the purpose ; the deficit between the amount so realized and the expenditure needed was contributed by the State, and, to add further to the municipal revenue, the old jail building in the town was handed over to the committee for conversion into a municipal market, and the daily bazar, which used to be held previously along the side of the main road in front of the Rajbati was removed there, to the decided improvement of the town both from a sanitary and from a utilitarian point of view. Regular inspection of foodstuffs was also made to ensure that no adulterated or deleterious food is offered for sale ; and so from the " unhealthy place " of Mr. Wylly's report, Baripada has become a notably clean and well-ordered town and as healthy a place to live in as can be found in Orissa.

CHAPTER XIV

The Maharaja as an Administrator (*continued*) —Development of Material Resources of the State.

With the combined objects of providing more work and ensuring the greater wellbeing and security of his people and of obtaining more money with which to carry out his plans for improvement, Maharaja Sri Ram Chandra let slip no opportunity for developing and exploiting the material resources of the State, and it must here be remarked that he had no selfish object in this desire to improve the State finances. For his personal expenditure he took only a modest sufficiency, a bare three or four thousand rupees per month. Practically the whole income of the State was spent from year to year in improved methods of administration, public works, and schemes of development, and so though in his time the revenue increased from about four lakhs to over three times that amount, none of it was wasted on vain show or selfish indulgence. His finance was conducted on sound lines. The budget, including the civil list with his own allowance as estimated for his requirements during the year, was annually considered and passed by his Council and was rigidly adhered to, while provision was made against future emergencies such as flood or famine by setting aside for investment each year such amount as was not required for current expenditure. At the time of his death the sum so invested on account of the State amounted to over eleven lakhs, all held in sound securities and drawing good interest. It was not unprofitably hoarded away in the treasury or in the form of ornaments and jewels, but was employed usefully elsewhere and steadily increasing until such time as it might be needed for use in the State.

The forest and mineral wealth of Mayurbhanj are its chief assets apart from the ordinary products of cultivation, and the Maharaja spared no pains to foster the development of these in the best and most profitable way. The forests had in bygone days been practically wasted, being ruthlessly cut down and burned for the extension of cultivation, or, where exploited for the production of timber, so hacked about and cleared away as to render them useless for any other purpose in future save the provision of firewood. In short, the methods then prevailing would in no long time have resulted in the complete disappearance of the jungles, as has happened in so many places in India, with the inevitable result of deterioration of the climate and soil, to say nothing of the loss to the people of timber for agricultural and household purposes and to the State of a permanent source of income. The Maharaja saw at once that it was necessary in the interests of the State and its inhabitants to prevent this disastrous possibility, and with this object set about the creation of a separate Forest Department. In 1894 he secured the loan from Government of the services of Mr. C. C. Hatt, Deputy Conservator of Forests, who drew up an exhaustive report on the forests of the State and prepared a preliminary working plan for a small portion of it, about 88 square miles. Thereafter a well-organised Forest Department was gradually formed to arrange and control all forest matters on the model of the forest administration prevailing in a British district. Prior to this systematic organisation, the revenue from forests never exceeded Rs. 30,000 per annum. Before the close of Sri Ram Chandra's rule, it had reached the sum of two and a half lakhs, and this not by ruthless and indiscriminate felling for sale nor by imposing on the raiyats excessive or unaccustomed charges for the wood they might legitimately require for use in their houses and fields, but by a sound system of royalty and export duties and by careful and scientific exploitation, through the granting of felling leases to approved contractors, chief of whom were Messrs. B. Barooah & Co., who, in the last ten years, have done more and better forest work in the State than any one else.

The income from timber, large though it is, is not nearly so great as it might be were better facilities for export available. In early days the Maharaja had tried to overcome this difficulty by working the forests himself, and for this purpose established a completely equipped saw mill at Bangriposi, near the principal jungles; but owing to the difficulty of transport the scheme ultimately proved unremunerative and was abandoned. It was with the object of providing an efficient means of export that the Maharaja in conjunction with Mr. Barooah formulated a project for extension of the State light railway into the Simlipal Hills, where the best and largest quantity of sal and other timber is to be found, and it was indirectly in connection with the advancement of this scheme that he met with the accident which resulted in his death. It would have been a source of intense gratification to him to have seen the inauguration and construction of this railway extension, which is now well on its way to completion and will, in conjunction with the lease of the whole Simlipal forest area to Mr. Barooah projected by the Maharaja and now finally sanctioned, open out an immense source of revenue and provide employment for numbers of people for generations, to come. The careful policy of exploitation combined with conservation initiated by him, will further result in the reafforestation of large areas previously denuded and the regeneration of forests already spoiled, and secure for the future not only a constant supply of timber for sale outside the State, but an adequate and perpetual provision for the household and agricultural requirements of its inhabitants.

As regards the mineral wealth of the State, it was known previously that valuable minerals existed, but up to this period only local use had been made of them. Rough utensils had been made of pot stone and soapstone and sold by the stone cutters at the bazaars in the neighbourhood. The Santhals employed the stores of red and yellow ochres for the decoration of their houses. The flagstones of the Kuliana quarries made good flooring for the State buildings and grindstones for the pounding of curry and spices. Gold washing afforded a somewhat precarious livelihood to a number of families in Bahmanghatti and elsewhere, and the local blacksmiths made a very good quality of iron from the ores which are found in abundance all over the State. But no one had hitherto done anything to ascertain the extent and value of these various deposits nor to develop their potentialities commercially. It was left to Maharaja Sri Ram Chandra to recognize their possibilities, and it is due to his fertile and versatile genius that a way was opened for and a beginning made of their full development.

In 1903 the Maharaja secured the services of Mr. P. N. Bose, B.SC., F.G.S., to make a geological survey of the State with the object of discovering the location and estimating the extent of deposits of minerals of commercial value. This survey was never fully completed, but enough was done to prove that the deposits of iron ore in particular were of enormous extent and almost unequalled purity. Negotiations were opened for leasing out the iron ore areas and a prospecting lease was ultimately granted to Messrs. Tata and Sons, who commenced boring operations in Gurumahisani and Sulaipat Hills in 1906. The field was visited in that year by Messrs. Perin and Weld, the American experts, who pronounced the ore to be of excellent quality, second perhaps to none in the Asiatic Continent. The supply was reported to be practically inexhaustible, the "floats" that were visible on the surface being sufficient for the consumption of a large number of years. Proposals for floating a company in England were then made, and a survey for a broad gauge railway to connect up the mines with the Bengal-Nagpur Railway at Sini was commenced in 1906. For various reasons, however, these proposals did not fructuate in their original form. Ultimately Messrs. Tata and Sons took up the flotation of a company in India, and in 1908 made survey and cleared jungle for the construction of the buildings and plant necessary to work the deposits at Gurumahisani. In the same year the final arrangements were made for the construction of a railway from that place to Kalimati on the Bengal-Nagpur Railway; and by 1911 everything was completed and work on the mines was in full swing. Now the Iron Works of the Tata Iron and Steel Company at Sakchi are the most important and largest single manufacturing concern in India, and they draw the whole of their enormous supply of ore from the Mayurbhanj State.

The other results of the geological survey showed that gold, mica, asbestos, steatite, ochres, limestone, kaolin, and building and ornamental stones of various kinds were to be found in Mayurbhanj. Of these the most attractive was naturally gold, but though this was found in alluvial deposits no trace of the original lodes was at that time discovered. Prospecting leases for the precious metal were granted to some persons, but it was found that the alluvial gold was not sufficiently rich to pay for extraction on a commercial scale. Prospecting parties are now at work trying to discover the original lodes and there is some hope of their success.

Prospecting licenses were also issued from time to time for exploration of the other minerals named above. Of these, soapstone, granite, and flagstones are the only ones that have been commercially developed so far.

Crushers and Siding, Gurumahisani Iron Works.

A Calcutta merchant took a lease of the soapstone and pot stone quarries and exports a considerable quantity of utensils and ornaments made of these minerals, and the Bengal Granite Company took a lease of the granite quarries along the Gurumahisani-Kalimati Railway and does considerable export. In 1906 a prospecting license for building and ornamental stones, limestone, ochres, and kaolin was granted to Messrs. B. Barooah and Patrick Gow. This firm exhibited a number of samples of these minerals at the Calcutta Industrial Exhibition and was awarded a gold medal for ornamental granite and a silver medal and certificates for the other exhibits, but so far no serious effort has been made to exploit these. It is hoped that their development may be made possible by the extension of the railway now under construction. As for the mica and asbestos mentioned in the geological report, further exploration is required to show whether or not these exist in workable form and quantity.

Mention must also be made of the Mayurbhanj Electric Scheme as showing the avidity with which the Maharaja seized on opportunities for developing his resources and the perseverance with which he investigated their possibilities. The scheme owed its inception to Mr. J. A. Martin, L.C.E., the State Engineer, and was based on the facilities offered by the natural formation of the gorges and falls of the Burabalong river for the generation and storage of hydraulic power. The river descends from the Simlipal plateau in two falls of nearly 600 feet and thence passes through a valley about 4½ miles in length, narrowing towards the end in the Kusumbandh gorge, the walls of which being almost perpendicular and of hard rock make an ideal spot for the construction of an enormous dam. A general survey of this natural available hydraulic power in the State was made in February, 1907, under the supervision of Mr. C. H. Douglas, A.M.I.C.E., and thereafter a careful survey was made of the Kusumbandh gorge and the water-power available throughout the year from the Burabalong falls. The results were so encouraging that the British Westinghouse and Electric Manufacturing Company executed an agreement in 1908 for the generation of electric power from this excellent source, the idea being to supply electricity to Calcutta and other centres, but the difficulty and cost of transmission of the current over such long distances and other hindrances prevented at that time the further development of the scheme, which, however, remains an active possibility of the future.

CHAPTER XV.

THE MAHARAJA AS AN ADMINISTRATOR (*concluded*) —PUBLIC WORKS—HIS CHIEF OFFICERS—APPRECIATION OF HIS WORK.

IT will be readily apparent that the many-sided activity of the Maharaja in his reform and elaboration of the administration and his development of the material potentialities of the State necessitated a corresponding activity of the Public Works Department to keep pace with the constant need for providing new and improved buildings, roads, bridges, the railway, irrigation works, and the like. Nothing is more striking in the growth of the State during the Maharaja's rule than the constant increase from year to year in the number and improvement of public works of all kinds. The annual expenditure under this head alone grew from about half a lakh at the beginning of the period to close on four lakhs at its close,—a sum about equal to the total income of the State at the time the Maharaja assumed control. From being a roadless tract without any buildings worthy of the name, the State was opened out with a network of roads connecting all places of importance with each other and with the outside world, and provided with good and substantial buildings for the accommodation of all branches of the administration and the residence of officers and their convenience on tour, so that it can now challenge comparison in this respect with any of its neighbouring districts and is far ahead of its sister States. It is not possible nor desirable to describe in minute detail the many useful works carried out by the engineering department, but a short sketch of the main achievements may prove interesting.

The main buildings erected for administrative and other purposes comprised a complete and commodious group of offices, well built, in stone, to accommodate the whole of the judicial, executive, and other departments at Sadar, which had heretofore been obliged to find cramped and unsatisfactory quarters in odd corners of the Rajbati and elsewhere. Good office buildings were also erected at the headquarters of each of the three subdivisions with the necessary complement of police stations, schools, and dispensaries. Quarters were built at Baripada for such of the higher officers of State who had no houses of their own, and were leased to them at a low rate of rent proportionate to their pay.

Reference has already been made to the magnificent King Edward VII. Charitable Dispensary at Baripada, the erection of which was in progress at the time of the Maharaja's death ; besides this there

Victoria Diamond Jubilee Institute, Baripada.

were six other dispensaries built in the State, of which five were substantial and suitable brick structures. The police station at Baripada, which was being remodelled and enlarged in 1911-12, is a fine building; and the jail, which is capable of accommodating over 300 prisoners calculated according to modern requirements of space, is as good and well-conceived a structure of the kind proportionate to its requirements as can be found in India. Besides all these and other edifices, there were over 30 inspection bungalows erected at suitable spots throughout the State for the convenience of touring officers and travellers. Mention must also be made of the fine High School at Baripada with its large lecture-room; and of the Victoria Memorial Institute, a picturesque building erected in memory of the late Queen-Empress, which comprises a fine hall, a good library and reading-room, and a most interesting museum wherein are displayed many relics of antiquity and samples of all the modern products of the State.

During this period 502 miles of road were constructed, of which 149 miles were metalled and 353 miles were gravelled or katcha roads; and such roads as existed from before were widened and improved, so that now it is possible to drive or motor to most parts of the State. The most important and costly means of communication, however, which was designed and carried out by the Public Works Department was the light railway from Rupsa to Baripada, the opening ceremony of which has already been referred to. It was very evident to the Maharaja that the State could never do justice to itself unless it had free access to the outside world for trade, and as soon as the Madras line of the Bengal-Nagpur Railway was opened he set about connecting it with his capital town by rail. The line, which is 32 miles long, was entirely constructed from State funds and by the State engineers, and reflects the greatest credit on the enterprise of the Maharaja and the skill of his staff. It gave the greatest possible incentive to the development of all kinds of activity in Mayurbhanj, and has added many times its cost to the prosperity of the people.

Another subject in which the Maharaja was keenly interested was irrigation. The surface conformation of the greater part of Mayurbhanj is such that, while it lends itself peculiarly to the construction of irrigation reservoirs and channels of all classes and dimensions, it is not possible to get the best results out of the higher lands unless means of irrigation are provided. Numbers of small earthen bundhs have been constructed by the raiyats themselves, the State paying such proportion of the cost as was needed to help them. Larger earthen bundhs with masonry outlets, too big and expensive to be constructed by the raiyats, were made by the Public Works Department and, taken together, irrigate a large area. But the Maharaja recognized that while such works were necessary and useful, they could never provide even a small proportion of the irrigation necessary to bring the greater part of the State under the best cultivation and secure the whole from the possibility of failure of crops through drought. So he contemplated and began the construction of a system of masonry dams with an elaborate network of canals and distributaries, of which two, the Baldiha and the Haldia Schemes, were nearly completed, at a cost of over six lakhs of rupees, by the time of his death. The main canal from the Baldiha reservoir is over 8½ miles long and the Haldia canal is over 6 miles long, and the two systems now irrigate 2,364 and 2,243 acres of land, respectively, and are gradually being extended. These schemes only formed part, however, of an extremely ambitious project which the Maharaja had in mind, namely, to dam the Burabalong river near the point of its exit from the hills and thence irrigate the greater part of the Sadar Subdivision. This project, while it will be very costly, is not only perfectly sound and feasible from an engineering point of view but will be a source of great profit, not alone from the revenue realizable but more from the tremendous increases in cultivation and improvement of land which will result, and will, moreover, secure a very large proportion of the agricultural land of the State from any possibility of failure of crops through drought; and though the Maharaja was unfortunately not destined to see his plan carried into effect, it is still being worked upon and there is every hope that it may be brought into full being at no far distant date.

It is not possible to refer to these evidences of the Maharaja's enterprise and energy without connecting them also with the name of Mr. J. Arnold Martin, L.C.E., who, appointed as Chief Engineer of the State in the time of Mr. Wylly, loyally continued to hold the office throughout the rule of Maharaja Sri Ram Chandra, and by his ability, energy and painstaking zeal practically created the Public Works Department of the State and was responsible for the conception, design, and execution of all the work carried out by it during this long period. As a leading member of the State Legislative Council, too, he added much to the soundness of its deliberations by his shrewd common sense and his great experience of the affairs of the State.

It is fitting also here to pay due tribute to the names of some other officers who have devoted the best part of their lives to the State, and without whose wholehearted assistance the Maharaja would not have been able to accomplish what he did. Mr. Kiddell and the part he played in forming the character of the young Chief and guiding him throughout his career have already been spoken of. Another officer with whom the Maharaja first came in contact at College in Cuttack was Babu Mohini Mohan Dhar, M.A., B.L., who was a professor in the Ravenshaw College and came to Baripada in the first instance as Judicial Adviser to the State and tutor to young Sri Ram Chandra in mathematics and science, and became in turn Superintendent of Education, State Judge, and then Dewan on the death, in 1906, of Babu Prasanna Kumar Ghosal, who had worthily held that post from the time of Mr. Wylly's management. Mohini Babu by his ability, and knowledge of law and procedure, had no small part in building up and maintaining the efficiency of the machinery of administration of the State, and continued to work for it to the best of his ability till failing health compelled him to resign, shortly after the death of his Chief. Among other officers the foremost is Babu Haridas Basu, State Judge, who by his conscientious hard work, his soundness of judgment and strong sense of justice, and the integrity and purity of his character, has won the regard and affection of all who have come in contact with him. Babu Nani Madhub Mukerjee, first as Auditor, then as Examiner of Accounts and eventually as Secretary and Examiner of Accounts, established the Financial Department. His premature death, in the seventh year of his service, was a serious loss and the work passed to the hands of his brother Babu Phani Madhab Mukerjee who, for nine years thereafter until the Chief's death, ably carried it on. Nor must one forget the names of the men who helped the administration in those early days when Mayurbhanj was not so accessible as it is now, nor its service so attractive. Among these were Pandit Govinda Chandra Mahapatra, tutor to the Maharaja when a minor and later senior assistant State Judge, to whom the Maharaja owed much educationally and otherwise. Babu Ram Narayan Sarangi, State Collector, who worked with thoroughness and uprightness in the Revenue Department almost throughout a generation; and Dr. Purna Chandra Gupta, the founder of the modern Medical Department. Last but of chief importance must be acknowledged, as the Maharaja himself acknowledged, the great assistance given to him by the various officers of Government who held from time to time the position of Commissioner in Orissa and Superintendent of the Feudatory States, and Mr. L. E. B. Cobden Ramsay, C.I.E., I.C.S., who, throughout the last seven years of the Maharaja's life, was Political Agent for the Orissa Feudatory States, and by his zeal on their behalf, untiring energy, and the soundness of his advice and readiness of his assistance, rendered incalculable aid to the Maharaja in formulating and carrying out his policy of reform and improvement on the best lines.

In 1911, Sir Edward Baker, Lieutenant-Governor of Bengal, while handing over to the Maharaja the

Sanad in which the hereditary title was conferred upon him, said:—" For more than twenty years your State of Mayurbhanj has been excellently managed under your own personal supervision, and your administration has always called for and evoked the cordial approbation of Government, and I trust your youthful successor will have the wisdom to follow in your footsteps." Just over twelve months later the Maharaja's career on earth was ended, but its results will live on in Mayurbhanj State. They may be fittingly summarised in the words of the speech delivered by the Dewan, Babu Mohini Mohan Dhar, at a meeting held in Baripada under the presidency of the Political Agent to consider a proposal to erect a memorial to the memory of the late Chief:—

"I knew him for about 24 years, first as my pupil at Cuttack and then as my master in Mayurbhanj, and very few knew him as intimately as I did, and I had the greatest regard for the dearly beloved Maharaja. He was a model ruler, a wise administrator, a noble man of high character, and an ideal gentleman. Justice, progress, and reform were the keynote of his administration. It is known throughout the length and breadth of Mayurbhanj with what care he dealt out even-handed justice and held the scales evenly between diverse classes and clashing interests. When Maharaja Sri Ram Chandra assumed the reins of office he found an income of a little over four lakhs, but at the present moment the income of the State is thirteen lakhs. Within a span of less than 22 years he increased the revenue three-fold, and he effected this vast expansion of revenue not by recourse to rackrenting, but by fair and equitable assessment. The administration was almost of a primitive kind when he took over charge, but at the time of his death his State, though small, was regarded as one of the best governed native States in India, and there are now well defined laws, rules, and regulations for every branch of administration. The whole administration was built up by him on British lines, and he has left it in a well-organised and highly developed State which met with the applause alike of the public and of the Government. He was recognized as a model ruler by the Government.... The good of his subjects, the development of his State, and reform of its administration were always nearest to his heart, and we all know what hold he had on the affection of the people. He considered himself an officer of the State and helmsman appointed by God. He considered himself the heaven-appointed trustee of the State. A Viceroy thus described what Indian Chiefs should be like: 'Their State is not their private property. Its revenue is not their privy purse. They are intended by Providence to be the working bees, and not the drones, of the hive. They exist for the benefit of the people, their people do not exist for them. They are intended to be the types, leaders, and examples.' To this description Maharaja Sri Ram Chandra Bhanj Deo fully answered and he came up to this ideal. He never spared himself and never wasted his time, and always worked hard in the discharge of his duties. He was so dutiful that even after the fatal accident which led to his death he wanted to hold a sitting of the Judicial Committee for the disposal of pending appeals, though both his hands were bandaged at the time and he could move about only with difficulty. With difficulty I could dissuade him from doing so.......

"His guiding principle in administration was to choose proper men and invest them with large powers and to combine the best advantages of constitutional government with the best advantages of personal rule. He never considered himself above law but, following the principle in vogue in British India, allowed his orders to be contested in the Civil Courts. His idea was that no man was infallible, and he gladly submitted to reversal of his order by his own Courts and with perfect equanimity admitted his own mistake when the matter went up in appeal to the Judicial Committee of which he was the President. Such cases undoubtedly were rare, but how many Chiefs in India can bear the idea of their orders being upset by their own officers. That he could do so bears indisputable testimony to his high-mindedness and breadth of view.

" Since his assumption of the Chiefship of Mayurbhanj, education has spread, administration has advanced, income has expanded, the material condition of the people has improved. A railway has been opened and big irrigation works and other important public works executed. He tried his utmost to develop the resources of the State. But for him the Tata Iron and Steel Works, of which the whole of India is proud, would not have been possible. Had he lived long enough to mature and bring into operation the grand electric energy scheme, that would have added another laurel to his fame. Had he not been cut short in the prime of his life, by the cruel hand of death, he would have accomplished many things more. Towards the end of his career the extension of the railway to Tarband and the establishment of the summer headquarters of the Lieutenant-Governor at Meghasani were uppermost in his mind. . . . .

" The Maharaja preferred his people to himself, and ability, character and merit to kinship. His most cherished idea in life was to work untiringly for the good of the land of his birth and he achieved no ordinary amount of success in that object, so dear to his heart. His high character, sound learning, varied experience, excellent state management, firmness of loyalty to the paramount power, received recognition from the political officers and the Government, and he was invested with full powers and was honoured with the title of hereditary Maharaja and with the first seat among the Orissa Chiefs at the last Delhi Durbar, and had he been spared longer further honours would have been conferred upon him.....................

" He was remarkable for the assiduity with which he devoted himself to the affairs of his small principality, and he personally attended to the business of the State with a devotion, fund of common sense, justice and impartiality, and a genuine desire for the good of his subjects, which made him loved and respected by all. The death of a ruler of his capacity and devotion is a great and irreparable loss to the people of Mayurbhanj. By his death Mayurbhanj has lost its most brilliant ruler, Orissa has lost its brightest jewel, and India one of its most worthy sons."

CHAPTER XVI.

MAHARAJA SRI RAM CHANDRA AS A MAN—HIS PERSONAL APPEARANCE AND MANNERS—HIS SELF-DENIAL AND SIMPLICITY—HIS SENSE OF DUTY AND JUSTICE—HIS LOVE OF WORK—HIS THIRST FOR KNOWLEDGE—HIS FINE CHARACTER.

" I was not born
" Informed and fearless from the first, but shrank
From ought which marked me out apart from men :
I would have lived their life and died their death
Lost in their ranks, eluding destiny."

THESE lines of Browning aptly describe the subject of these memoirs. Reserved almost to a fault, modest and unassuming, yet he felt that for him to drift with the current could never be. One who knew him intimately all his life recalls his saying during a conversation on the subject of his aims and ambitions :—" If only it could be done without drawing so much attention to oneself." But he conquered his natural shyness, faced his duty boldly, ignored much of the hostile criticism and opposition directed against his measures, and left Mayurbhanj something like he had dreamed and desired it should be.

Maharaja Sri Ram Chandra was not only an exceptionally able and efficient ruler but a man of rare private virtues, which won for him the soubriquet of Rajarshi, or Saintly Chief. He was deeply enshrined in the hearts and affections of his people, not only because he was a sympathetic Chief, "a guide, philosopher, and friend," but because he was also a prince of men, with a lofty character and moral excellences which surpassed even his intellectual abilities, brilliant though these were. To practise virtue out of necessity, to renounce luxury owing to poverty, and to be unaffected by temptations where there are none, may be commendable but is not heroic; but to annihilate oneself and elevate one's soul in the midst of ease and plenty, to resist temptations at every step, is a brilliant triumph which requires heroic effort and heroic strength, and therefore commands the unstinted admiration and heartfelt homage of all. He who can do this is no ordinary man, but a personality, endowed with supreme moral force and lofty ideals. He is not a recluse but a man of the world, yet above it. His greatness has a unique grandeur because it is the result of unique strength. Such a man was Maharaja Sri Ram Chandra Bhanj of Mayurbhanj. He had his failings and shortcomings as other men have, for no one is perfect in this imperfect world of ours; but his failings were so few and insignificant that the public never heard of them at all and hence they regarded him as an ideal man.

"Tall handsome and majestic, the late Maharaja was by birth, as well as by instinct, a true ruler of men" wrote the "Bengalee" in an obituary notice. "The Indian Daily News" of the 23rd February, 1912, said, "The Maharaja of Mayurbhanj was a man who took a deep interest in his State—an Indian Raja of the new type. Educated at the Ravenshaw College like an ordinary person, he behaved like an ordinary gentleman, never gave himself airs or led any one to believe that he was a Maharaja. Singularly modest and unassuming, he had one intense desire, to develop Mayurbhanj." And in the "Indian Mirror" of the same date we find, "He bore a spotless character and possessed a deep religious disposition. His simple and unostentatious disposition and his sweet temper were equally remarkable. His courtesy and hospitality, together with his inborn sympathy for every human and righteous cause, made him a lovable figure among all classes."

His manner, indeed, was so charming and unassuming and his modesty so great and unaffected, that in his presence one forgot the stiff artificial rules of conventional etiquette, and could talk freely with the Maharaja as with an ordinary gentleman. He knew no pride or condescension, but was affable and accessible to all, even to the humblest chaprassi or to the poorest labourer. His humility was the outcome of his natural temperament as well as his fine culture, hence his greatness was always marked by gracefulness too.

His self-control was remarkable. "I knew him for 24 years," said the Dewan, "but I never saw him lose his temper." On one occasion the late Babu Nani Madhav Mukherji, his Secretary, seeing the Maharaja carrying his bag himself, scolded his servant Radhu, who lagged a few yards behind, and reminded him to look after his duty lest his master should get angry. "The Maharaja never scolds us or gets angry with us," replied Radhu. "If I fall asleep at night, and if he has any occasion for me, he wakes me up with a gentle touch or generally does not disturb me at all."

One day, during the life-time of the first Maharani, the Maharaja sat at breakfast, but, just as he was about to eat, he suddenly stopped short and left the food untouched. To the Maharani's enquiry as to what was the matter he replied that, if she promised not to take anyone to task, he would explain. She gave the promise as desired and the Maharaja then showed her a small cockroach which had accidentally got mixed up with the rice. He had to go without breakfast that day, but he did not mind it, and attended to his duties as usual. The Maharani was very gentle and good natured and never scolded any one but, seeing that her husband had to go without breakfast, she very gently asked the cook to be more careful in his duties in future.

Full of shame and fear the cook hurried to the Maharaja's office and with folded hands said," May your Highness excuse my shortcoming this time." The Maharaja kindly replied, " Why have you come to me? Did I say anything to you? Go and attend to your duties with a little more care in future. All people are more or less liable to such shortcomings occasionally." At dinner time that night the Maharaja remarked in good humour to his wife, " Women cannot keep their word. You promised not to say anything about it to anybody yet you could not keep your word."

It must not be supposed from the above incident that the Maharaja was wanting in ideas of discipline. On the contrary he was a strict disciplinarian and spared not even the highest officers of the State if he found them guilty of any laxity of duty; but he possessed in full that inestimable quality of the truly just man of being able to discriminate between unintentional omission and wilful negligence and to apportion punishment accordingly

To quote again from the Dewan's memorial speech, " His self-denial had hardly a parallel. At Baripada he passed his days and nights in a small ill-ventilated bedroom, which was even partitioned with paper. For some years he felt the necessity of building a suitable palace for himself, but at the time of preparation of the budget he always put it off for the future as he could not deprive the administration of funds for his personal comfort. The Maharaja was a rich man no doubt, but he led a simple and unostentatious life and lived almost like an ascetic. His ideal was plain living and high thinking."

"The Statesman" of 23rd February, 1912, in an appreciation of the Maharaja writes, "He was a man of enlightened views, a strong business ability, and progressive ideas. He was at the same time simple and retiring and never refused help to any deserving object." In commenting on the simple life he led, Babu Khirode Chandra Roy Chowdhuri, M.A., Editor of the "Star of Utkal" said, in an article in his paper of 2nd October, 1912: "In simplicity he surpassed all his brother Chiefs; a dhoti worth a rupee, a mirjai, and a chadar, was his ordinary dress. In addition to this he used to don a panjabi when he went out. One day at the Howrah Station we met the Maharaja at the booking office buying a ticket. In surprise we asked, 'Where are your men, why are you buying your ticket yourself?' The Maharaja smiled quietly and looked on all sides and retorted, 'Where are your men; why are you buying your ticket yourself?' We said 'Your life, Maharaja, is much more valuable. You are the Maharaja of Mayurbhanj worth thirteen lakhs; I live from hand to mouth; what a comparison?' The Maharaja replied, 'Khirode Babu, I have got what I have by an accident of birth.

Your reputation is self-acquired. What a comparison!' We were non-plussed..........

"In his private life the Maharaja was a Rajarshi; his princely income he spent either for the benefit of his people or for supporting philanthropic movements, himself living the life of an ascetic. He was a vegetarian and a strict teetotaller."

As regards his vegetarianism we are reminded of an incident which occurred on one occasion when the Maharaja was a guest of the humble writer at the marriage ceremony of the writer's daughter, when, according to our family custom, no provision of fish or flesh was made for the guests. The Maharaja was served only with ordinary vegetable food, hence we were taken to task by our elder brother for not making some special provision of fish or meat for him, and made the apology that the Maharaja was a vegetarian. The Maharaja forthwith corrected the statement saying, "No, no, I am not a strict vegetarian; under medical advice I sometimes have to take fish or meat, though I am more fond of vegetable diet." This shows how eager and prompt he was to prevent any false impression from gaining ground. One more anecdote illustrating his simplicity in diet will be interesting as well as instructive. On one occasion, during a tour in the Panchpir Subdivision, he became the guest of the then Subdivisional Officer, Babu Anukul Chandra Roy, M.A., B.L. Anukul Babu called the Maharaja's cook and asked him what provision he had for his master. Madhu opened a small bundle which revealed some mushrooms and pieces of dried cauliflower and some boris. "Is that all, Madhu?". "Yes, sir" replied he. "Of course we have rice, pulse and a little ghi besides, but no fresh vegetables." "You may keep them Madhu, for future use; now do what I tell you," ordered Anukul Babu and he provided the cook with a quantity of potatoes, brinjals, beans, and other vegetables which he grew in his small kitchen garden. When he sat down to dine the Maharaja was surprised to see so many dishes of fresh vegetables, which he had not tasted so long, as he had been touring in the mofussil, and said "Anukul Babu, why have you made all those elaborate arrangements for me? I had everything with me." Anukul Babu told the writer that he only with difficulty refrained from replying "I have seen your provisions, Maharaja, but your meanest subject dines on better fare."

Not only was he simple in matters of diet and dress, but in all his actions. Babu Nagendra Nath Banerji of Mayurbhanj told the writer that on one occasion he invited the Maharaja to a prayer at his humble cottage. It was an open air meeting and the guests sat in Indian fashion on the grass in the garden, only one stool being provided for the Maharaja who turned up a little late—when the prayer had already commenced. Alighting from his carriage he left his shoes at the gate and walked barefooted to the place where prayer was going on. He got the stool removed and sat on the grass like the rest and the charming surroundings of lovely and sweet scented flowers, the bright stars twinkling overhead, the delightful calm and soft breeze of the May evening, filled his heart with rapture and he was soon absorbed in his devotions.

His strong sense of duty and love of impartial justice is well illustrated in a case which occurred a number of years ago. A servant of the Rajbati was prosecuted for some criminal offence and was sentenced to a term of imprisonment by the then State Judge. Thereupon the master of the said servant, a very influential member of the Raj family and close relation of the Maharaja, flew into a rage and rescued the prisoner from the custody of the police. When the Chief was consulted as to what was to be done, he, without hesitation, said that the law was no respecter of persons and there could not be one law for the people and another for the privileged class. Accordingly legal proceedings were instituted against that influential relative, and the law took its due course. The case created quite a sensation in Mayurbhanj, and henceforth it was felt that the authority of the Court was a power not to be set at defiance by any one, however high his rank or position might be.

This regard for the dictates of duty was equalled by his love for his work. Nobody in Mayurbhanj worked harder than the Maharaja himself, and even the minutest details of all matters of administration were at his fingers ends. " Those who knew him," says the "Amrita Bazar Patrika," " knew it well that he laboured harder for the good administration of his State than his meanest servant. Work was his idol." In fact he overworked himself and when warned by his medical advisers he used to say "Man is born to work." Babu Hemendra Nath Singh, B.A., who at one time served in the State as Settlement Officer, in an article in the " Nabya Bharat," relates that the Maharaja used to say to the officers that they might enjoy leave, but he could not, because the people did not allow him any, meaning to say that their welfare was entrusted to him, and so he was not entitled to enjoy any rest for himself. It was this conscientious devotion to his work that came in the way of his long desired travel in foreign countries. He felt that he could not reconcile such a long holiday with his feeling of duty and he was only enabled to take it when, by leaving the State in the charge of the Political Agent, he could feel that it would be well cared for in his absence.

It was remarkable that, in the midst of the multifarious duties which engrossed his attention, he could find time for study, yet he was an extremely well read man and loved to keep his reading up to date. It is related that once, when reading a critique of a newly published philosophical work, he was asked whether he would get a copy. "I have one," he replied. "It came by last mail. I ordered it in advance." He studied everything that was useful and took an interest in everything that was good. His favourite study in later life was metaphysics, but law, history, economics and general literature received no small share of his attention and he was a close student of the Sanskrit Upanishads and other religious books. The late Babu Narendra Nath Sircar, M.A., B.L., pleader of Cuttack, who was much respected for his sterling honesty and purity of character, once told the writer that on one occasion he had a long and very agreeable conversation with the Maharaja, in which among other things metaphysical subjects were discussed. Narendra Babu had made a thorough study of Hamilton's metaphysics, and, on incidentally referring to some point dealt with in that work, he was greatly surprised to find not only that the Maharaja grasped it readily, but that he was thoroughly conversant with the book and freely dealt with some of its most important and intricate details. Another Indian gentleman who had studied economics in the American universities, while talking about economic conditions of different nations, found to his astonishment that the Maharaja was quite up to date in modern economic ideas as propounded by the best writers, and noticed a copy of Walker's Economics on the Maharaja's table, which was evidently there for use and not for show. An eminent English counsel of the Calcutta High Court once spoke very highly of the Maharaja's legal knowledge and acumen, and expressed his agreeable surprise to see that a layman could handle in such a masterly way the intricate points of law, as the Maharaja had done in writing a particular judgment in a case tried by him.

His interest in history was particular as well as general, and it was his earnest desire to have compiled a complete history of the Mayurbhanj State. With the object of collecting and compiling materials for this he engaged in 1906 the services of an Archæologist, Babu Nagendra Nath Vasu, M.R.A.S., whose researches brought to light many objects and customs of antiquarian interest dating from the 2nd Century B.C. to about 1600 A.D. Nagendra Babu published a critique of these discoveries and their bearing on the Jain, Buddhistic, Indo-Scythian, and Tantric influences in his "Archælogical Survey of Mayurbhanj," a book of great interest and value to students of the religious history of India.

In social matters the Maharaja's views differed from those of the orthodox community and he called himself a progressive Hindu. He had liberal ideas about social reform and considered that effete orthodoxy hampered national progress, and he felt that in dealing with social questions the broader principles of humanity should outweigh all other considerations, though he never advocated social revolution all at once.

"In religion," to quote again Babu Mohini Mohan Dhar, who knew the Maharaja as intimately as any man did, "he was an Adwaitabadi or non-dualist, according to whom there are not two but one. The Adwaitabadis believe in the oneness of the Universe, and they maintain that one Infinite Being is the only existence which is manifesting itself in all these phenomenal forms. According to them there is no 'I' or 'you,' it is all one, and that 'I' and 'you' and God and everything else are all one. They say that the Infinite cannot be two. If the soul be infinite there can be but one soul and all these ideas of various souls are not real. This is the essence of the abstruse Vedanta philosophy, of which the Maharaja was an ardent student. This Adwaitabad is difficult to conceive, but Sri Ram Chandra had occasion to tell me that he could realise this oneness. Whatever his own religious inclination might have been, toleration was his principle in religious matters and he made no distinction of caste or creed in dealing with his people." In one of his letters to the Dewan he wrote, "I regard myself as a Hindu, or Arya, or whatever else you may call it, and my religious convictions are essentially those of Hindu Vedantism as read in the light of Western Science and Philosophy."

"He approached very near the ideal man, in appearance, in character, and in manliness." So writes the "Amrita Bazar Patrika," of Calcutta. In the administration report of the Orissa Feudatory States for 1911-12, Mr. Cobden Ramsay, the Political Agent, wrote: "I deeply regret to have to record the death of the Feudatory Chief of Mayurbhanj; his loss is a lamentable and irreparable one to this Agency; both in his personal and public capacity he was ever animated with a spirit of high mindedness and a most earnest endeavour to do his duty to all alike. His death has been a grievous loss." These appreciations of his lofty character would be corroborated by all who knew him. Wordsworth's "Character of the Happy Warrior" might have been written of Maharaja Sri Ram Chandra :—

"Who is the happy warrior?
  "It is the generous spirit
"Whose high endeavours are an inward light
  "That makes the path before him always bright.
"Who with a natural instinct to discern
  "What knowledge can perform, is diligent to learn;
"Abides by his resolve, and stops not there
  "But makes his moral being his prime care.

* * * * *

"More skilful in selfknowledge, even more pure,
  "As tempted more; more able to endure,
"As more exposed to suffering and distress;
  "Who comprehends his trust and to the same
"Keeps faithful with a singleness of aim."

His most fitting epitaph is written in the lines of the immortal Shakespeare :—

"His life was gentle, and the elements
"So mixed in him Nature might stand up,
"And say to all the world, 'This was a man'."

APPENDIX.

THEISM: THE NATION'S NEED.

I.

LADIES AND GENTLEMEN,

The first words are naturally those of greetings. Here in the Metropolis of Modern India, have met once more, men of culture and piety, from many parts of the land.

From Madras that played an honoured part in the Religious Revival of Mediæval India and is still an honoured Home of Culture, of Religious and Social Reform—from the Punjab where Nanak, the first Apostle of Harmony, preached the Gospel of Pure Theism long ago—from Bombay the Beautiful and Maharashtra the Mighty—from the far off classic Soil of Sind—and from different parts of our dear *Bangadesha* are come thoughtful, earnest, devout souls in sympathy with the Theistic Ideal, to take their part in the activities and enthusiasms of the Theistic Conference.

The spectacle of such a representative gathering is certainly a source of comfort (shall I not add?) of strength—to all who strive to-day to extend the cause of Rational Piety and Spiritual Religion. It sustains us in our spiritual strivings, and charges with energy the hope that the great Vision of a National Church for New India may be verified at no very distant date. Here in this hall are brought together men who love spiritual life more than the *creeds* of religions—and faith and fellowship more than *forms* of faith. Here is an illustration of what may be spoken of as a Religious Federation broad-based on inter-religious co-operation. For the deepening of spiritual life—for a frank and free communication of thoughts and convictions and religious experiences—for a re-wording of the vital truth of *spiritual sympathy* which bears all and beholds in all an image of God's Truth growing 'with the process of the suns'—for re-interpreting the thought that Modern India needs the sustaining force of Spiritual Theism—are met together all who will for four successive evenings take part in this Conference of Religion.

In sending forth the word of greeting and in setting forth the spirit and scope of this Conference, I am urged, as the Representative of the Reception Committee, to indicate, in brief, the *Basis of Theism* no less than to give some expression to what I consider to be the *National Significance* of the Larger Faith in us.

II.

The questions which will soon engage the attention of this Conference are connected with the spiritual and moral welfare of Mother-India. To my mind, there is no question, so significant to-day as the one about the religious re-awakening of this country. Spirituality and asceticism are the natural endowments of our countrymen ; but under the burden of a material civilization which has come upon us, they stand in some danger of losing their hold. I am far from decrying the blessings which modern civilization has conferred and may still confer on us ; but it is meet that our moral progress should keep pace with it. True progress consists in the *harmonious development of all departments of human activity,* and not in that of one at the expense of another. If religion be neglected, or ignored, there will surely set in an atrophy of a vital part in the *race-organism.* The glory and greatness of Ancient India were centred in her religion, and the glory and greatness of Modern India will also be in her religion. *Let the memory of the past be an incentive to spiritual progress, and not a cloak to hide our present shortcomings.* The time may come when the West will seek inspiration from our religion and philosophy, even as we are now receiving inspiration from Western Science and Art.

Recently India had the privilege of hearing the message of the West from Dr. Cuthbert Hall, the eloquent and sympathetic American divine. Let me quote a passage from his recently delivered lectures : "May the day never come when the East inebriated with the wine of modern culture and dazzled by the appliances of modern civilization shall move from her high seat of vision, forget her prophets of the invisible, barter her great inheritance in the unseen and bow down before the perishable idols of the present age, the unconsecrated gods of a passing hour." These are weighty words, and it would be well worth the while of this as well as of future generations to bear them in mind.

III.

At the present moment we see around us activity in all directions. Questions regarding political rights, industrial development, social reform, etc., are engaging universal and serious attention, but the religious problem stands still. It does not seem to receive sufficient recognition and thought.

The reason for this indifference is not difficult to find. Things which meet the eye, and meet our *immediate sense-wants* easily receive our attention ; the more we fix our attention upon them, the stronger the spell they throw around us. But realities unseen *appear* remote, and do not, therefore, readily lend themselves to our comprehension ; they are unnoticed except by those thoughtful few who have their gaze fixed upon the present as well as the future. Then again, in our, commerce with the external world, from the very date of our birth our notions and ideas have become so fixed and rigid that spiritual truths remain unperceived and unrealised.

But it does not follow that things which remain behind the veil are of less moment to us than the things of *sense-experience*. Surely, if the human soul is to retain its spiritual richness and vigour, things spiritual must no less be its concern than things material. To realise this,—to realise the transitory character of terrestrial existence,—to realise that religion is the informing principle of all true and unselfish life,—that it is the motive power which is behind all moral actions in individuals no less than in nations, ***a contemplative mood is absolutely essential.*** So it was that "*Yoga*" and "*Dhyan*" were held in high esteem and were regarded as preliminary steps along the path of religion in Ancient India.

The value of contemplation is fully recognised by philosophers in the West. Mr. Balfour, the ex-Premier of England, who in the midst of the most engrossing duties of a world-wide empire yet found time to attend to philosophy, writes in his book, "Foundations of Belief": "Yet after all it is in moments of reflection that the worth of creeds may best be tested; it is through moments of reflection that they come into living and effectual contact with our active life. It cannot therefore be a matter to us of small moment that as we learn to survey the material world with a wider vision, as we more clearly measure the true proportions which man and his performances bear to the ordered whole, our practical ideal gets relatively dwarfed and beggared till we may well feel inclined to ask whether so transitory and so unimportant an accident in the general scheme of things as the fortunes of the human race can any longer satisfy aspirations and emotions nourished upon beliefs in the Everlasting and the Divine." It is to the absence of the contemplative mood in this age of stress and strain that the daily declining interest in religion is due.

IV.

When I use the word religion, I do not mean the *nominal religion of convention* which a son inherits from his father, nor the *formal religion of Scribes and Pharisees*, which a man may put on as a coat or cloak on particular occasions, but the *personal religion* which is the quickening principle of all thought, of all life. It is this religion which leads man on to unselfish and noble deeds and gives him strength in the hour of trial or temptation. It is this religion which led the devoted band of Christian martyrs to face the most dreadful tortures which human ingenuity could invent, with a grace and resignation which, while receiving assent, challenges belief. The most outrageous persecution acted but as fuel to the fire. The power of kings and emperors failed to arrest this tide of *living religion.* Fire and sword were powerless again the bulwark of faith. Upon this solid foundation of sacrifice and devotion the great edifice of the Christian Religion is built.

The rise of the Mahomedan Religion affords a typical illustration of the *power of religious faith.* From an insignificant and unknown place in Arabia religious fervour spread over the length and breadth of two continents.

Our own country affords innumerable instances. From the hoary past, of which some record remains down to the present day, every generation has seen heroic bands of enthusiastic souls leaving hearth and home and all that man holds dear in their search after the unseen. " No more thorough mortification of flesh has ever been attempted than that achieved by the Indian ascetic anchorites." And nowhere perhaps has the Divine Presence been more vividly realised. In all countries and in all ages have appeared men who have exemplified in their lives the tremendous influence which religion exercises over human lives and affairs.

Undoubtedly there have been numbers of men in all ages and in all countries over whom religion has had very little influence. It is no more my purpose to deny this fact than to deny that there is evil in this world. It is true also that in the name of religion much human blood has been shed and many atrocities perpetrated; but *religion has been unfairly charged with the sins of irreligion and the excesses of its votaries.* And the large fact lives that in the history of the world and in the lives of individuals religion has played an all-important part, and that *living religion wherever found is a force to be reckoned with.* Even Mr. Mill, a critic so hostile to the claims of religion, is forced to admit the beneficent part it has played in the past. In his essay on "Utility of Religion," he says: "It is in short perfectly conceivable that religion may be morally useful without being intellectually sustainable, and it would be a proof of great prejudice in any unbeliever to deny that there have been ages and that there are still both nations and individuals with regard to whom this is actually the case."

We sometimes hear persons say that the influence which religion is said to have exercised over human lives is really due to the great moral power which has all along been under its command, that a " little reflection " will show that religion receives the credit of all this influence which really belongs to morality ; in other words, these persons maintain that in this rationalistic age a rational ethical system and abstract moral ideals are quite enough for the guidance of human conduct and that theistic belief is no longer necessary to nourish them. The *raison d'être* of ethics is a much disputed point, and the moral ideals of different philosophers have varied ; but, avoiding hair-splitting discussions, one may say with truth that man *can distinguish intuitively what is right from what is wrong*, can feel also an *impulse* to do what is good and to avoid what is bad. But if the basis of our moral impulse be only a shadowy moral ideal and nothing more, the question suggests itself :—Has that basis *sufficient strength* to stimulate the impulse of *self-fulfilment ?* I believe not. Is an *impersonal moral ideal* sufficient to reform the drunkard and the profligate ? I believe not. It is when morality is quickened by a living theistic faith that such miracles of moral reform take place. The history of ages supplies innumerable instances of sinners reclaimed by Goodness and re-born in the Kingdom of God. Of such instances we have some personal experience, and the experience of universal humanity has shewn that *moral power gains in strength in proportion to the intensity of religious faith.* Prof. William James, the greatest of living psychologists, in his refreshing and humorous style, writes thus in his book, " The Will to Believe :" " The capacity of the strenuous mood lies so deep down among our natural human possibilities that even if there were no metaphysical or traditional grounds for believing in a God, man would postulate one simply as a pretext for living hard and getting out of the game of existence its keenest possibilities of zest. Our attitude towards concrete evils is entirely different in a world where we believe there are none but finite demanders from what it is in one where we joyously face tragedy for an infinite demander's sake. Every sort of energy and endurance of courage and capacity for handling life's evils is set free in those who have religious faith. For this reason the strenuous type of character will, in the battle-field of human history, always outwear the easy-going type, and religion will drive irreligion to the wall. It would seem, and this is my final conclusion, that the stable and systematic moral universe for which the ethical philosopher asks is fully possible only in a world where there is a divine thinker with all-enveloping demands. If such a thinker existed his way of subordinating the demands to one another would be the finally valid casuistic scale, his claims would be the most appealing, his ideal universe would be the most inclusive realizable whole. If he now exist, then actualized in his thought already must be that ethical philosophy which we seek as the pattern which our own must evermore approach."

V.

Buddhism is sometimes cited as an instance of a purely ethical religion which without belief in God, has held sway over one-fifth of mankind for centuries together. Ethical enthusiasm, moral idealism, spirit of self-sacrifice are, certainly, characteristic of Buddhism; and to call Buddhism a *purely ethical religion* is, I submit, a blunder. Buddha himself stands as the *personal evidence* of *the Religion* of the *Spirit ;* else would he have never been for ages accepted as the *Tathagata.* Indeed in the *Sadhamma Pundarika* (" The *Lotus* of the *Good Law* ")* we read of the Infinite and Eternal Person, the Self-existent Spirit ; and, further, that Sakya Muni was but one of His recurring manifestations. Think, again, of the Buddhist *Belief in the Hereafter,* and of the suggestive *Doctrine of the Deed* (Karma) interpreting the universe as a *moral organism* nourished by unfailing Righteousness. Surely, the idea of Religion is immanent and operant in this Buddhist conception which interprets the world as woven on every one of its " seven sides," with *Wisdom* and with *Moral Law.* Surely, the Buddhist may well exclaim :—

" Thou dost preserve the stars from wrong,
And the most ancient heavens through
Thee are fresh and strong."

A religion pledged to such a faith cannot be called a purely ethical religion. Scholars differ as to the exact significance of its doctrine of *Nirvana.* What to a Western scholar may mean annihilation, to the mystical oriental mind is, in very truth, a transcendental state of existence free from desires and pains —a state of being which passeth human understanding. It is true, some

---

*Cf. Translation by Kern, Sacred Books of the East, Vol. XXI.

schools of philosophical Buddhism never laid special emphasis on the doctrine of God ; but may not this very shortcoming explain why it did not appeal to the soul of India, and why in countries where it still exists the place of God has been taken by Buddha himself ? That Buddhism was, in some of its implicates, pessimistic is true ; but a religion which believes in a Hereafter and in a Living Original of moral order, can by no means be stamped as atheistic. The true significance of Buddhism yet remains to be unfolded ; and a profound and critical study of its literature may yet throw an interpreting light upon its inner meaning and its larger message.

Our age has seen the birth of a purely ethical religion, *viz.*, the religion of humanity, which in its zeal for rational piety, has enthroned the *abstract idea of humanity* on the seat consecrated to God. This is an outcome of the religious instinct asserting itself where belief in the Godhead has been undermined by a narrow rationalism. As a purely ethical religion, "*its ideal lacks the note of infinitude and mystery.*" It is but a makeshift of the imagination which can never retain the charm which reality alone possesses ; nor can its pseudo-divinity arouse adoration and stir the springs of deep devotion. That its ideal is not acceptable to the human heart is proved by its lack of adherents. To bolster up religion without a basis of belief in a Living God is very much like trying to keep a watch going without its hair-spring, and is therefore destined to fail.

VI.

My object in taking up so much of your time in treating religion from a stand-point which may be called *pragmatic* rather than *utilitarian* is this—that in this age of science and rationalism, in the hurry and bustle of modern life, when people seem to have no time for contemplation, when *value-judgment* is so easily understood and appreciated, it is well to give prominence to the *value of religion as the motive power to all* noble deeds, as the soul of morality and as the *dynamic principle* which has changed sinners into saints. But value or utility is not the *ground* upon which religion lays her claim. She rests her claims on her own *intrinsic worth* and not on some *extrinsic* attribute of *utility*.

The greatest privilege which we enjoy in this age is *freedom of thought*. It is the greatest achievement of the Modern Age. The marvellous conquest of man over the secrets of nature, the marvellous inventions by which the forces of nature are pressed in the service of mankind, are some of the results of the spirit of freedom working on the physical plane. The greater regard for the suffering of living creatures, the greater efforts for their alleviation, the greater respect paid to the opinions and beliefs of others, the larger enthusiasm for Universal Humanity are some of its results working on the moral plane. No longer are we required to submit to fetters forged by age or fixed by tradition. No longer is reason—'the candle of the Lord'—a captive in the prison-house of dogma. But if the freedom we enjoy is great, *our responsibility is also great.*

In an age when authority had a greater hold, understanding was willingly lent in captivity to ecclesiastical authority. That was, perhaps, a necessity of the age. Things, I think, have changed ; we are now in danger of running to the other extreme, and *mistaking license for freedom.* In this age understanding is regarded as the one supreme standard of religious belief; understanding is regarded as the 'open sesame' of truth.

But there be other ways in which the self functions as well as in the way of understanding. Let us gladly recognise the importance of understanding (*verstand*) ; but we must not be blind to its limitations. We must bear in mind that intense concentration of mind and perseverance are indispensable to science,—that the greatest discoveries of modern science have demanded not simply *investigation* but also '*scientific imagination, intuition, insight, synthetic vision.*' A flash of intuition is felt by the mind of a genius ; and following the track of the flash, he *sees* a scientific truth, he makes a discovery which, perhaps, posterity alone may verify. Again, induction—the great instrument of science—itself rests on *rational faith ;* without this rational faith in the *uniformity of nature* the whole structure of science will tumble down, and human life itself will be paralysed. It is then, not the application of the intellect alone, but the *functioning of the self* as a *whole* which leads to the discovery of truth. If this is the case so far as physical science is concerned, what must it be as regards metaphysics, the science of sciences ?

Dealing with ultimate problems with a subtlety all its own, metaphysics does not seem to find much favour in the present age. But if the divine truth is to be known, if the Temple of pure thought consecrated by the genius of man unto the Unseen is to be understood, the study of metaphysics is essential. Truth, whether seen by Sankaracharjya or Fichte or Hegel, is one and universal. And the master minds of the world whose thoughts have dwelt on the Unseen have left us a valuable asset in their speculations bearing on ultimate reality.

Matter and force, the idols of physical science, perplex the mind when metaphysically approached; still more is the mind perplexed when it strives to apprehend the Transcendental, the Absolute, the Self-sustaining all human souls. The human soul must rise above the distractions of this earth—must enter into the calm and clear atmosphere of contemplation—must have a pure mind, a devout heart, a delicate conscience,—must pass within the Sacred Circle where alone may come some golden gleams of the Mystery whose shadow rests over all. If the soul is to have God-vision which Jesus and Chaitanya had, it must also have *the faith of Jesus and the love of Chaitanya*. If, then, we approach the Transcendental with our methods of experiment and physical observation and, perhaps, with a mind whose natural instincts and impulses have suffered havoc from a narrow rationalism—if we do this and find nothing,—we do but prove the blindness of *rationalistic understanding* and not that the Light streaming through the Mystic Sense is delusion and darkness.

VII.

The mystical experience of prophets and seers and saints of all lands and all ages is a fount of inspiration to the weary soul; and so our debt of gratitude to the *spiritual fathers of mankind* is immense. Infinite are the ways of the Eternal of interpreting Himself to man, if man will but have the eye to see and the heart to feel; specially rich, in this regard, is the experience of those God-intoxicated souls, who in a growing spirit of self-surrender gave their all to God and lived and had their being in Him; they illustrate the ancient truth that in proportion as a man *ascends* does God *descend* to meet him. When nature clothed with beauty presents herself to us and the mind is filled with awe or with sweet repose—when on reading some rhythmic, soul-subduing poem, or hearing some hymns of glory in the holy hour of dawn, the mind is filled with holy thoughts—or when in the midst of a devout congregation attuned to worship sublime, the soul is lifted to higher heights of the spirit—it is *then* that the hand of God touches the spring of the human heart, and the *jivatman* enters the blessedness which passeth understanding.

It is however in the moment of sorrow—of that deep sorrow which is the lot of man—when heaven and earth seem an utter blank, an empty void,—when the heart is wounded with many wounds,—when the mind finds no rest except in the cry of a pure and passionate prayer to God,—it is in that critical yet blessed moment that man hears distinctly a Voice whispering words of hope and love; then, too, he receives support and strength to bear all the suffering which the world can inflict; then, too, he begins to feel that sorrow is a blessing in disguise, that *suffering is a sacrament*. He who has *realized* all this holds in his hands a key to the enigma of life. The world, to such an one, is no longer a fortuitous concourse of atoms, but a divinely designed habitat of living beings; human beings are no longer the playthings of blind fatalistic forces, but the "*offspring*" of God after His own image.

Mysticism is a subjective experience of the mind when it is in touch with the spiritual; *and the experience is vivid and real no less than is the experience of the phenomenal world*. It has been felt by many in all lands and in all ages; though medical materialism has long confounded it with hypochondria and other morbid mental phenomena! But mystic experience, I am glad to note, is receiving thoughtful attention to-day; and Lombroso has lived to know that *saints* are not *mere neuropaths*. The New Psychology is already striving to study, in a larger light, the *Problem of Personality*; and as more and more of the phenomena bearing on Intuition, Genius, Exaltation of the senses, of Ecstasy, Conversion and other varieties of Religious Experience, come to be investigated, the world will receive a scientific justification of the experience and influence of what the mystic calls the *Spiritual World*, of what the late Mr. Myers called the *met-ethereal Environment*. Then, too, shall come to us a better knowledge of the convictions and consecrated contents of the *larger consciousness* with which the Mystic is in daily-deepening contact. In this connection, let me voice the sentiments of all and say that our grateful thanks are due to Dr. C. C. Hall for his invaluable and illuminating exposition and defence of mysticism. India is the land of Yoga; here mysticism is fully understood and appreciated. Mysticism runs in our veins. The Upanishads and the Vedanta—are they not one wondrous outpouring of the Mystic Song? The Himalayas and the Indian ocean *invite us to mystic communion*, as they once invited the Rishis of our Ancient Past. Are you ready to give response?

Let the closing words of my address be the words of him in whom the Mystic Sense was keen and strong—the words of one of the very greatest of Modern India—of the late lamented Rev. Protap Chunder Mozoomdar:

"How is it, that in spite of all the great Western books and the Hebrew books which we love and revere, we have an inalienable love and reverence for the great sacred books of India? It is not a foolish patriotism. Rationality is indeed higher than nationality: and when the two conflict, nationality must go to the wall and rationality prevail. But here rationality and nationality strike up the same tune. We are perfectly reasonable, perfectly logical, when we extol the spiritual insight of our ancient sages which not only we shall develop and maintain, but the whole world shall have to accept. The spiritual genius of India, the deep seeing of the Hindus, shall not die. It is the wisdom which the East once taught the West and will teach once again. O Sons of Rishis, followers of the revered ancestors, your souls rapt up in traditional bond have lost altogether the genius and inspiration which are your legitimate inheritance. Nature is steady, creation is the same living divine thing, but our ears are dull, our understandings dead. Possess once more the wisdom of your fathers, read between the verses of the tenth mandal of the Rigveda and your Theism, call it by what name you will, will be your salvation."